From Boardroom
to Baby

*A Roadmap for Career Women Transitioning
to Stay-at-Home Moms*

Kristin M. Helms

This edition first published in 2017 by Career Press,
an imprint of Red Wheel/Weiser, LLC
With offices at:
65 Parker Street, Suite 7
Newburyport, MA 01950
www.redwheelweiser.com
www.careerpress.com

ISBN: 978-1-63265-125-9
Library of Congress Cataloging-in-Publication Data
Names: Helms, Kristin M., author.
Title: From boardroom to baby : a roadmap for career women tran-
sitioning to
    stay-at-home moms / Kristin M. Helms.
Description: Wayne : Career Press, 2018. | Includes bibliographical
    references and index.
Identifiers: LCCN 2017034804 (print) | LCCN 2017046956 (ebook) |
ISBN 9781632658814 (ebook) | ISBN 9781632651259 (paperback)
Subjects: LCSH: Stay-at-home mothers. | Work and family. | Self-
realization | Conduct of life. | BISAC: FAMILY & RELATIONSHIPS /
Parenting / Motherhood. | FAMILY & RELATIONSHIPS / Parenting /
General. | BUSINESS & ECONOMICS / Careers / General.
Classification: LCC HQ759.46 (ebook) | LCC HQ759.46 .H45 2018
(print) | DDC
    306.874/3--dc23
LC record available at https://lccn.loc.gov/2017034804
Cover design by Howard Grossman/12E Design
Cover illustration by Askold Romanov/istockphoto
Interior by Gina Schenck
Typeset in Minion Pro and Corbel

Printed in Canada
MAR
10 9 8 7 6 5 4 3 2 1

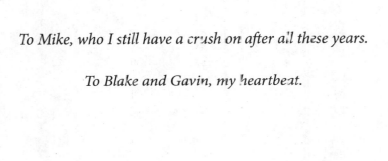

To Mike, who I still have a crush on after all these years.

To Blake and Gavin, my heartbeat.

Acknowledgments

First, thank you to my fifth-grade teacher, Mr. Scates, who gave me confidence in my writing capabilities by telling me that one day I would become a published author. That seed he planted within my soul turned into a lifelong dream, and is now a reality.

Thank you to Waverly Fitzgerald, who taught me how to write a stellar non-fiction book proposal that would get noticed (it worked!); to my literary agent, Jill Marsal, for taking a chance on a newbie author; and the entire team at Career Press for believing in this project and welcoming me into their family of authors.

A big thank you to my aunt, Karen Simms, for all of her incredible collaboration throughout writing this book, and to all of the stay-at-home moms who offered up their personal, heartfelt thoughts and stories throughout these pages.

Thank you to my family (Mom, Dad, Jaclyn, Jaimie) and close friends who have always been cheerleaders for my writing and my creative journey.

To my parent-in-laws, Donna and Randy, who flew out to California to watch my kiddos for an entire week while I hunkered down and wrote the majority of this book; and to my dog, Tucker, who kept my feet warm during those late nights writing.

To my husband, Mike, for his unwavering support and love through this rollercoaster ride, and to my children, Blake and Gavin—my tiny muses—for giving my life purpose and joy.

Contents

Introduction

My Story

Tap, *tap, tap.* The sound of my mother's electric typewriter cut through the thick summer heat as I carefully struck each key with my pointer finger. The machine usually acted as a fun toy for my sisters and me when we played "office," but now it took on a more serious role in printing my very first business cards for my very first business. I was 10 years old and I was on a mission.

Before the ink was dry, I distributed my cards to every doorstep in my quaint neighborhood in East Sacramento, California. My babysitting and pet care service ran cheap, and it wasn't long before I had numerous clients and a full calendar to fill my summer break between the fourth and fifth grade. My early start as an entrepreneur pointed toward the path my life would follow throughout the next 20 years— my work ethic and internal drive for success seemed to be a part of my DNA.

When I was 14 years old and of legal age to work in California, I proudly marched myself into the Baskin-Robbins down the street from my house and got my very first job scooping ice cream; I was ecstatic at being able to earn a pay-check all my own.

For the next 16 years, I always had a job, sometimes two. I put myself through college selling ad space in San Diego State University's school newspaper by day and waitressing by night. Four years later, I had obtained a bachelor of arts degree in communication with an emphasis in advertising. By the time my college graduation rolled around, I had re-ceived a handful of entry-level sales and marketing job offers. I accepted the one with the highest salary and best benefits, and dedicated myself to ascending the corporate ladder. Motivated by success through career, salaries, bonuses, and prestige, I was living the corporate dream one promotion at a time.

Flash forward 15 years. At 29 years old, I was sitting pretty at my dream job as the marketing manager for one of Hyatt Hotels' largest properties in the world in San Diego, California. My days were filled conducting creative meet-ings, lunching with editors from high-profile magazines, managing photo shoots, writing ad copy, and rubbing shoul-ders with city bigwigs at oceanfront networking events. It required long hours but it was fast-paced and interesting. I loved every second.

Then I got pregnant. It was planned; my husband and I were pushing 30 and eager to start a family. I remember shutting the door to my office as I left to go on maternity leave. *See you soon,* I thought to myself.

I never returned to that office and that life. Instead, I did what millions of other career women have done and veered off of my career track, settling into a new life as a stay-at-home mom. The transition from a thriving marketing career to a life based on domestic responsibilities was a shock to my system—a once well-oiled operating machine, now falling apart at the bolts. I was grateful to be spending every moment possible with my beautiful daughter—there was no way I could fathom leaving her. But I also had to find a new source of self-worth and self-identity.

My old work hustle didn't translate to my new role at home, and I didn't understand how to feel fulfilled in life by cleaning the house and doing laundry.

Some days I felt bored and envisioned the real world, full of vibrant life, adult conversations, and worldly accomplishments, dancing outside of my home, where I felt stuck inside a life I didn't recognize. Other days I felt overwhelmed caring for a tiny infant who demanded every ounce I had to give. My emotions, outlook, and new life felt foreign and out of my control. *Why was this new existence so wildly different from what it seemed to be on the surface?* My picture of the stay-at-home life, gleaned from watching TV shows and hearing some of my relatives praising this lifestyle, was a startling contrast to my reality. *Maybe it was me,* I thought. *Maybe I wasn't cut out for this path after all.*

I was smothered by guilt every time I felt less than grateful about spending time with my precious baby. I knew another mother who would sob during her commute to work every morning because she wanted to stay home with her children but couldn't because of financial reasons—that woman had no choice. And there I was, wishing I felt more fulfilled in my new role while I was lucky to witness my daughter's first smile and first laugh.

To battle the guilt I felt, I came up with a plan: I would pour my whole self into motherhood. If I was going to stay home, I would be the best stay-at-home mom the world had ever seen! I muzzled the warning voices in my head, suppressed my need for an identity outside of mom, and ignored every red flag along the way. I became a good housewife: I cooked three carefully planned meals a day, kept the never-ending laundry cycle in motion, researched developmental exercises and games to play with my baby, and convinced myself that this was what "staying home" looked like.

This plan worked for a couple of months—two-and-a-half long and trying months to be exact. I quickly learned that this way of mothering wasn't sustainable. By failing to take care of my own body, mind, and soul, and giving 100 percent of myself day in and day out, my tank ran dry. I had nothing left to give to my family. I was exhausted, depleted, and felt like a failure again. Strike two.

About six months into my new role as a stay-at-home mom, I realized something had to give. Either I had to return to the workforce and find a daycare for my daughter, or I needed to look at my new life as a stay-at-home mom in a different light. Clearly, the stereotypes of stay-at-home moms I'd witnessed in the media were misrepresented. I needed to redefine the role on my own terms. I would stop trying to fit the mold of what I thought a stay-at-home mom was, and I would intentionally recreate the role in a way that worked best for my daughter, my husband, and most importantly, *me*.

From what felt like the deep, dark rock bottom of my new life, I sparked a fire within my soul that ignited a new definition for my "stay-at-home mom life." While I obviously still needed to keep our household running through chores and cooking, the terms of my new-and-improved role also offered empowerment, self-improvement, creativity, reflection, and in turn, better parenting for my daughter.

Instead of looking for validation, praise, and a sense of success from the outside world, I taught myself how to look for those same things from within. Just because I was now a stay-at-home mom without a career didn't mean I wasn't also the same strong, capable woman who had always believed in myself—from the time I was 10 years old, passing out business cards, to the 30-year-old running a marketing department for a Fortune 500 company. In this new season of life, I was now a mother, but I was also still me.

I set intentional goals for myself, rediscovered who I was at the core, reprioritized my life, and continued to learn along the way. Most importantly, I allowed myself grace and gave myself a fair chance to succeed in this chapter of my life as a modern-day woman and a new mother.

What to Expect from This Book

Picture your career life as a journey, hiking in the woods along a mountain trail. You've been climbing this path for a while now—catching your stride at certain points, overcoming some obstacles and setbacks along the way—but you always knew where you were heading: onward and upward, following the trail.

Now pretend you've made the life-altering decision to pivot off of your career path and begin blazing your own journey through the woods as a stay-at-home mom. The journey that lies ahead of you is not well defined. In fact there is no path at all, just open woods. You're not sure how life will be without the trail laid out in front of you, but you know you want to experience the beauty of nature in its purest form, up close in person.

Leaving stability and the known, you pivot and head into the woods.

Now freeze that moment in time. The pivot point is what this book is going to focus on: the transitional time from a sturdy career to the all-consuming, self-reliant journey as a stay-at-home mom.

When you first veer off of the trail, into the unknown woods, you experience contrasting feelings: thrill, excitement, pure joy, magic, fear, uncertainty, and perhaps a longing for the familiar trail again.

And you start to question yourself and your decision to leave the well-established trail. *If you're not climbing the mountain along the trail anymore, where are you going? Will you be able to navigate through life without the trail? How will others view you for leaving your trail after you've come so far? Will you ever be able to find another trail again? Will you want to?*

And it's all mixed into one swirling, twirling reality for a finite period of time, because eventually you will learn how to navigate through the woods on your own. Of course there will be storms to weather and obstacles to overcome, but you'll journey on. There will also be sunny, magical days when you're thankful you're not on the structured trail anymore, because now you're close enough to appreciate the subtle beauty of nature you can only witness from this level of involvement: milestones and details you probably would have missed from the trail.

• • • • • • •

This book is intended as a compass for career women turned stay-at-home moms as they navigate the transition period between career and life at home raising children. This book was written for women who are considering leaving their careers to stay home, or women who have already resigned from their jobs and are looking for encouragement and guidance in their new roles.

This book refuses to partake in the mommy wars between working mothers and stay-at-home mothers nor does it proclaim that one path is better than the other. As mothers, we all make the best decisions for our own families and specific circumstances. I have the utmost respect for working moms, and some of my closest friends and family members are hardworking mothers. But this book isn't for them. This book is for the women who have opted out of careers and chosen to become stay-at-home moms and who are looking for support and conveyance as they make the transition into their surprisingly complex new existences.

I'll share stories and insight from my personal voyage—the hard stuff and the good stuff—and provide tools and exercises for you to accomplish along the way. I suggest you keep a journal or notebook close while you read along so you can complete the exercises found within each chapter. These exercises are key in helping you define your unique values and goals as a stay-at-home mom.

The brilliant and insightful Karen Simms, a licensed mental health counselor, will also weigh in on certain topics, providing "counseling advice" and guiding you through your unique passage into a fulfilling life as a stay-at-home mom.

Karen has more than 10 years' experience working with individuals through many of life's transitions, helping them find empowerment, fulfillment, and their authentic voices.

Lastly, each chapter will conclude with affirmations. These are provided for you to read and use however you see fit: recite them to yourself out loud, print them out and hang them on your bathroom mirror, or simply keep them in the back of your mind for future reference.

In order to fully embrace this new path for yourself, I'll ask you to forget all the stay-at-home mom stereotypes you've absorbed over time. Those aren't real life. And if they were real at some point in time, they're now outdated. Through the next several chapters we'll explore ideas that will help you break through those stereotypes and allow you to create an exceptional life that honors what is unique about you and your family.

Embrace this new venture and make it your own.

Because this is your life, too. Because you are a capable, strong woman. Because you are a loving mother. Because you are more than "Mom." Because life is meant to be lived through meaning and purpose. Because what you do as a stay-at-home mom matters. Because you matter.

Section 1:
A Leap of Faith

Chapter 1

Choosing to Stay Home:
Calculating Circumstance + Values + Self

*"What lies behind us and what lies before us are tiny matters,
compared to what lies within us."*
—Ralph Waldo Emerson

Mothers are made over time; built from the ground up, brick by brick, composed of a million different magical moments, sound bites of laughter, fear, tears, and a love that knows no limit. The existence gradually sinks into our souls and settles into our bones, starting from the second we see two pink lines on a pregnancy test. It continues to spread through our veins and heartbeat, until it consumes our very being. Somewhere along the journey it reaches our brain where we finally comprehend it entirely: *I'm a mother. I've created life.*

This moment of realization is different for every mom. One woman may feel the weight of this role as soon as she finds out she's pregnant. For another woman, it's the moment her baby is placed on her chest after delivery. And for many, it takes months after having a baby to feel connected to the title "Mom."

Regardless of when it reaches our brain, we can all recognize the magnitude of the revelation when it hits us: This is the most important role of our lives. The biggest responsibility. All of our deepest fears and brightest accomplishments live within this existence. And we're forever changed. A shift in thoughts, priorities, and lifestyle takes over at our very core and our decisions are made with new perspective and a new sense of accountability.

• • • • • • • •

I jolted upright at the faintest sight of dawn creeping through the bedroom blinds and jumped out of bed with an adrenaline kick stemming from not wanting to go another second on this earth without knowing my fate; *was I or wasn't I?* The signs were there—I had stopped the little pink pill more than a month ago, my usually very-regular period was missing in action, and I had convinced myself that my jeans were fitting much tighter than normal.

I grabbed the pregnancy test from my bathroom drawer and unfolded the direction booklet, studying the step-by-step diagrams while examining the white plastic stick. My late-night googling session the evening prior had informed me that the most accurate pregnancy results were obtained from a morning urine sample, when it was most concentrated. I had no room in my brain for a faulty test or a wish-washy result. *I needed results and I needed them now!* I held the stick in my urine stream for exactly five seconds and prepared to wait the three agonizing minutes for the science of it all to calculate. But after a quick 30 seconds there they were—the two pink lines that changed my life—clear as day: *I was pregnant.*

I floated on cloud nine back to our bed and gently nudged my husband—poor chap fast asleep and not prepared for the early-morning revelation that awaited him. His eyes fluttered open and focused on the stick I held just inches from his face. A giant smile spread across his face and we hugged in disbelief. *We did it! We made a baby!*

Throughout the next hour or so, we smiled and cried and said "Oh my god!" way too many times. We briefly discussed the logistics of calling my ob-gyn and scheduling an appointment. We agreed not to tell anyone but our parents for the time being. It was all so exciting!

And then we continued life as usual. We got dressed, ate breakfast, poured coffee, went to work, and made small talk with coworkers at the water cooler, all while harboring our gigantic secret. Then we fought rush-hour traffic on our way back home that afternoon, cooked dinner talked about our future as a family of three, watched our favorite TV show, and crawled into bed. A full 24-hours with business-as-usual. On the surface, we appeared to be the same—unchanged by the news. But even on that first day, still filled with routine from our pre-baby life, I felt the start of a shift within.

Throughout the next few months, two pink lines turned into a blob on an ultrasound picture with a rapid heartbeat.

The blob turned into a tiny alien baby with phalanges. The tiny alien baby turned into a larger, kicking (possibly kangaroo), baby in utero.

Nine months felt like 18 while we prepared (as well as first-time parents can) and waited for our tiny human to grace us with her presence. The nursery design, curated on Pinterest and executed through careful paint colors, wallpaper, and furniture arranging, was complete. Baby girl clothes were prewashed and organized by size and then color hanging neatly on soft pink mini-hangers in the closet. Swaddles, diapers, wipes, and lotions, along with more confusing things like NoseFridas and snot suction bulbs filled our wicker baskets lined with white linen and perfectly tied bows. A new breast pump along with foreign and intimidating tubes and flanges were ready and waiting for my first go at extracting milk. The car seat was installed in the back of our new SUV (which we bought after a tearful goodbye to my unpractical sporty sedan) and was double-checked by a local fireman to confirm every buckle and harness was in place. We were overly prepared and my Type A personality proudly checked all of the boxes on my detailed "Prep for Baby" list.

But there was one question that still loomed over us, one big box left unchecked: childcare. Would it be me or would it be some stranger who would take care of our new baby while I returned to work after maternity leave? Some days, I would make the decision to return to work; *how could I let go of my dream job after working hard to reach that level?* Other days I would decide to stay home; *how could I leave my precious new baby?*

Just two weeks before my due date, I vowed to wait and see. I couldn't possibly make such a large decision without first understanding what I anticipated to be complicated feelings after birthing a tiny human.

A couple weeks later, as I gently rocked my newborn back to sleep while rubbing her tiny back, I could feel my priorities shifting completely in one direction; I was spellbound in love. I knew I couldn't return to my job and leave her for 10-plus hours every day.

My husband and I did our due diligence while making the final decision and all signs pointed to me staying home: We had no immediate family nearby to help with childcare and the thought of leaving my new baby with a stranger for the majority of each day felt like having the wind knocked out of me. We were stable enough financially to live off of one income, although we'd have to tighten and cut back spending in some areas. And having both been raised by stay-at-home moms, we found real value in that lifestyle.

So I answered my looming childcare question with a final decision: "I'll stay home." And we checked that last box off the list.

Although I was physically prepared for my new role, confirmed through checked boxes and an organized nursery, I didn't expect the emotional transition that ensued as I embarked down my new path. I mistook my willingness to put my career on hold for complete understanding of my new position.

Blindsided by the change of pace and the pesky feelings that rocked my self-esteem, I had a startling revelation:

I had forgotten to consider how much my sense of "self" was founded on my work life.

Complicated decisions

It's the question that crosses every new mother's mind: *Should I leave my baby to return to work, or do I stay home with my child and pivot off my career course?* The question itself is complicated because it's laced with emotion and guilt. It feels unnatural to leave your baby, but if you enjoy your work and career, it feels unnatural to leave that life you've built for yourself. So how do you organize and prioritize your feelings and thoughts into something that makes sense? How do you ask yourself the right questions and reflect on your answers in a meaningful way?

....

Counseling advice

"The rest of this chapter lays out wonderful questions to ask in order to come closer to making this big decision. Notice your self-talk as you navigate these questions and your answers. Often we will hear in our heads what we 'should' or 'should not' do, and then we can feel shame or guilt when we want to push against these 'shoulds' and 'should nots.' Try replacing the should/should nots with the words 'I want' or 'I don't want' and notice how that feels. Does that bring you any more clarity? Also, notice the feelings that come up with the questions. Do some resonate more

than others? Are you noticing fear, excitement, joy, guilt? All of the above? With loving-kindness, explore these feelings and thoughts a little deeper. Are they attached to an 'old story' you have about yourself or parenting? Are these stories true? What do they tell you? Remember to breathe and take a break if you feel stuck or overwhelmed." —Karen Simms, mental health counselor

Circumstance + values + self

Considering **circumstance + values + self** is a helpful starting point when making the decision to stay home or return to work after having a baby. By diving in and exploring each of these factors separately, weighing the contents of each, and then looking at them combined, you'll likely catch a glimpse of where your heart and priorities lie. However, if you're looking for a clear-cut answer or a perfectly calculated equation that results in a definite answer, you won't find it here. Life is not always black and white; it's filled with uncertain gray areas and surprising colors— much too complicated to draw finite conclusions from a simple exercise.

But as you stand at this fork in the road and organize your thoughts into these three components, one path may start to appeal to you more than the others, revealing a natural course that seems to better fit your life: your personal circumstances, values, and self.

Exploring circumstance

Possibly the easiest part of the equation, considering your circumstances, is simply acknowledging your realities. There's little room for interpretation when you crunch the numbers and evaluate if you can live off one income. Of course you can get creative and decide to cut back in your spending or consolidate in order to make it work off of one income, but you probably already have a pretty good idea about what sort of financial support you'll need to run your household.

You also know for certain whether you have trusted friends or family in town that may be able to help with daycare if you return to work. And if you don't, you can research cost-effective and trust-worthy daycare or nanny options in your area.

"As I did not have any retired relatives capable of watching my new baby, I also looked at the cost of childcare in my state, realizing that after daycare costs I'd bring home barely anything for the full work week I'd spend away from my little one." —Marisa Svalstedt

Exercise: Identifying circumstances

After compiling some of the facts of your personal situation, you'll be able to clearly list your realities in this exercise. Consider the following and make a list with your answers:

Financial

- Crunch the numbers. Can you live off one income?
- What do you need to give up or cut back on in order to make the numbers work?
- How will life change for you and your family if you make less money every year? (Less family vacations, less dinner out, and so on.)

Childcare

- Do you have any close friends or family in the area who could help with childcare?
- Research daycares, interview nannies, and other childcare options. Do you trust the options you have in your area? Do any seem like a good fit?
- Write down the pros and cons of each childcare option.

Time Away

- How many hours per week did you work pre-baby? How much overtime?
- Is there flexibility in your role to work less or part time?
- Is there flexibility in your role to work remotely or flex-hours?
- How far is the commute to your office? What is traffic like during travel times to/from work?
- Calculate how many hours in total you'd be away from your child/children each day. Is the amount of time away something you're comfortable with?

- Does your job require travel? If so, how many days per week/month/year?
- Who will help care for your child during your travel time?

....

"My former job was wonderful in many ways. But it was also incredibly demanding. More than 50-hour work weeks, global travel, meetings upon meetings, and endless scores of emails. My husband's job was no less demanding (traveling every other week for 80 percent of the year), so it wasn't far into our human-raising journey that we realized we had to recalibrate. We desperately needed more balance, more flexibility, and more moments to actually breathe and enjoy the crazy gift of parenting. Our life at home was evolving and, as a result, our approach to 'work' needed to evolve too."
—Samantha Cronin

....

Exploring values

When I was pregnant with my firstborn, I wrote a list of hopes and dreams for my daughter and her life. It was important to me and my husband to lay the foundation for these values while she was young, before outside influences materialized. I still read this list often as it also acts as a parenting guide for me—a nice reminder of my larger parenting role beyond the daily duties of changing diapers, feedings, and cleaning.

My Hopes and Dreams for My Daughter

Kindness

I hope you never forget your roots.

I hope you stay down-to-earth and never think the world owes you anything.

I hope that if you want something, you work hard to obtain it.

I hope you're not afraid to get dirty, go camping, and play sports with the boys.

I hope you appreciate the small things in life that money can't buy.

I hope you never take sunsets, beaches, and the ocean for granted.

I hope you don't take yourself or this life too seriously.

I hope you'll never judge anyone at first glance.

I hope you keep your balance—life will try to teeter-totter you in extreme directions.

I hope that if you end up regretting something, you find a way to fix it enough so you can find peace within yourself.

Grace

I hope that you make wishes on shooting stars, dandelions, and pennies tossed in fountains.

I hope you handle this life with grace, through the good times and bad.

I hope, when you are young, that you believe in fairy dust, magic wands, and all things make-believe.

I hope you keep your manners and poise—it's amazing how far they'll get you in life.

I hope you notice and appreciate nice gestures by others.

I hope you are optimistic and always look at the glass as half full.

I hope you keep a sense of class and dignity about you, always.
I hope you recognize natural beauty.
I hope you build a strong enough wall around your heart so you don't get taken advantage of, but weak enough so the right person will be able to tear it all down.

Power

I hope you have a diva side (just to keep others on their toes).
I hope you have just enough edge to take the leap.
I hope you dance when it rains, laugh when you fall, and speak your mind when it counts.
I hope you have a fiery side, only when it's necessary.
I hope you chase your dreams.
I hope that you define your own success and then stop at nothing until it's obtained.
I hope that you never let anyone kill your spirit.
I hope you have confidence but not arrogance.
I hope you're not afraid to stand up for what you believe in.
I hope you know that you're as good as any boy, often better.
I hope you never settle.

....

"I had children so I could be a mother. To me, that meant raising them, passing on my morals and values, connecting with them, and spending time with them. —Beth Robinson
....

Exercise: Identifying values

Write down a list of values that are most important to you while raising a child. If it helps, write down your hopes and dreams for your child, revealing the values you want to instill in him or her.

It's important to note that you'll be able to accomplish these goals and instill these values whether you stay home or return to work. This exercise is simply to get you thinking about what's important to you on your journey through motherhood so you can determine how each path looks with these goals in mind.

....

"I felt a stirring in my heart to a greater call, to intimately shape this little being entrusted to us." —Amanda Ortega
....

Exploring "self"

This was the missing piece in my decision to stay home and the one factor that this book will explore in great depth: your "self" as a stay-at-home mom. *Can you picture it?* The external obstacles are widely discussed and usually expected: little sleep in the beginning, constant breastfeeding or bottle feedings, messes and tears. But it's hard to foresee the internal obstacles and know how to navigate the emotional journey this path holds. (I hope the chapters that follow will accomplish this).

Exercise: Identifying "self"

Write down characteristics that best describe your personality and your sense of self. Consider:

- Are you type A, highly organized and scheduled, or are you more relaxed with a "go-with-the-flow" type of personality?
- What makes you feel important?
- What makes you feel accomplished?
- What are you doing when you're happiest?
- What motivates you?
- Are you an extrovert or introvert? In what ways?
- What are your three closest friends like?
- When someone asks you about yourself, what's the first thing you say? Is it your job title or is it your hobbies, love for food or travel, and so on?

....

"My heart and soul are my children. I am not wired to be a working mom." —Michelle Nelson
....

Your answers to these questions are not a Magic 8 Ball that will tell you to stay home with your children or return to work. I've met thriving stay-at-home moms who had type A personalities and equally stellar stay-at-home moms with type B, C, and D personalities. This exercise will simply make you aware of what you need for yourself along whatever parenting course you choose. This list will also be helpful to reference throughout the remainder of this book.

"I never thought I would become a stay-at-home mom even when I was pregnant. It actually never crossed my mind. I loved my job as a CPA and had worked hard to get where I was in my career. However, all that changed after I had my son. It is a cliché, but for me, everything changed. All of a sudden my career was not as important as it used to be." —Melissa Clayton

Reflection

Read through your answers from the questions in this chapter, starting with circumstances, then values, and then self. Looking at all of this information together, what stands out the most?

Now pretend you've decided to return to work, and read your notes through again: How do your words resonate with you as a working mom? Are you happy in this life? Is your family thriving in this life?

Now pretend you've decided to stay home with your children and read through it all a third time, asking yourself the same questions: How do your words resonate with you as a stay-at-home mom? Are you happy in this life? Is your family thriving?

If simply considering your options is not enough to give you clarity, try living through an entire day as if you had made one decision, noticing what is different and what might shift. Then live the next day as if you had made the other choice. If one day is not enough, try living with one choice for a week, and the other choice for another week. Notice how you feel.

As with most big life decisions, you'll never be 100 percent sure you're making the right choice. You can do your best to foresee the obstacles and triumphs in each direction and then make an educated decision, or more accurately, a leap of faith.

....

Counseling advice

"With any choice or decision we make, we give up something and we gain somethig. Building a foundation of self-love and self-compassion can create a soft, safe space to navigate a difficult decision. With this in mind, allow yourself the space to grieve what you may give up with your decision. Give yourself permission to explore and express the feelings that come up with the letting go and saying goodbye to what you are giving up. And, again with self-compassion, embrace what you will gain and allow it to hold joyful space alongside the grief of what you have given up. This is the wholeness of your experience and how you feel."
—Karen Simms, mental health counselor

....

A compass

Since this book is an internal compass for new stay-at-home moms, we'll assume you've made the decision to put your career on hold (for a finite or infinite amount of time) and stay home with your child/children. Even if you're still undecided but leaning toward staying home, read on. The next chapters will unfold a map through the transition from a career to a life at home. We'll uncover all the obstacles along the way (some pebbles, some boulders), and help clear the path as you blaze your unique journey through motherhood as a stay-at-home mom, full of happiness, success, and self-discovery.

I know you're accustomed to looking at the world through the eyes of a nurturer, always putting others, especially your children, first. As mothers, that's what we do best. But in the next few pages I'll ask you to flip the lens and look inward. Who are you at the very core? What makes you happy and what makes you upset? What are your best traits? What parts of yourself do you need to work on? How do you value others and how do you feel valued? And how can we channel all of that into creating the best version of yourself for your child/children, your partner, and you in your new role as a stay-at-home mom?

Are you ready? *Jump.*

Affirmations

After making your decision to stay home, read the following affirmations and let them sink into your soul:

- I am making the best decision for my family.
- With grace, I embark on this new journey through motherhood.
- I grow through tough times and relish in the good times.

- I make this role my own. I have the power to create a beautiful life.
- I parent with intention and do my best to instill our family's important values in (insert child's/children's name(s) here).
- I am a mother but I am also (insert your name here).

Chapter 2

Eulogy for Your Career Self

*"You can't start the next chapter of your life
if you keep rereading the last one."*
—Unknown

Going from a high-paced marketing career to life on the home front with a newborn felt awkward. It was like running on a treadmill for 16 years—music pumping, blood flowing—and then the power went out and I was suddenly standing still, in complete silence. For me, standing still is always scary; I like to be moving, planning, doing. Consequently, in the first few months of my time at home, when I didn't know where to go, what to plan, or what to do in my new role, I'd often look back to my old career life. In some ways, I felt like I still had one foot in my past career life and one foot in my new life as a stay-at-home mother—it felt unstable.

Looking back, I wish I had completely closed the chapter on my old career self before fully emerging into life as a stay-at-home mom. By frequently looking in my rearview mirror, trying to catch glimpses of my past life and my identity that lived within that existence, I wasn't allowing myself the room and focus I needed to adjust to my new role at home. I wasn't giving my new reality, as a stay-at-home mom, a fair chance to blossom and thrive.

I soon realized that in order for me to truly appreciate my time at home, I needed a sense of closure on my career (at least for the time being). I needed to redirect my attention to the present and future as a full-time mom. Closure didn't mean forgetting who I was and all that I had worked for throughout my life. For me, closure meant taking a long hard look at myself in my present state—the good, the mediocre, and the straight-up ugly—and identifying what aspects of myself I wanted to keep, what I needed to improve upon, and what I wanted to toss as I moved into my new phase of life, at home with my precious baby.

Keep what you need

I gathered up the parts of myself that I knew I couldn't live without and mentally kept them a priority as I moved forward. It was important for me to *keep* three aspects of myself as I started down my new path as a stay-at-home mom:

1. **My drive toward goals.** I knew if I didn't set goals for myself in my new role, I'd feel lost and begin questioning my purpose. I thrive off of setting goals and striving to reach them. Although my goals as a stay-at-home mom looked strikingly different than my past career goals, the simple act of setting some and working toward them kept my motivation in high-drive.

2. **My need for structure.** I also needed to keep some form of structure within my days, months, and years. I knew my type-A personality wouldn't survive long without at least a little bit of organization, albeit the chaos, during my time at home. While I would learn to become more flexible (because, as we all know, mom life is full of curveballs), whatever loose structures I was able to set around my new life allowed me to function better as a mom.

3. **My need to express myself creatively.** An important one for me—I needed to keep some creativity in my new role as mom. In my past marketing job, I was able to exercise my creativity daily to compose ad campaigns, design brochures, and implement marketing strategies. I knew that leaving that job would cause a creative void that would need to be filled with some sort of outlet outside of "just mom."

Improve yourself

Next, I singled out the characteristics about myself that I knew I'd have to really work on in order to succeed as a stay-at-home mom—the parts of myself that needed fine-tuning for this next season of life. The two areas I wanted to *improve* upon were:

1. **Patience.** Because my past career was fast-paced and required juggling multiple balls in the air, I simply didn't have the time to deal with anything nonproductive. I often cut right to the chase during meetings and phone calls, sent direct emails with clear instructions or questions, and worked within a high-functioning, powerhouse of a team that churned out copious amounts of quality work. In that role, impatience was actually a quality that worked to my advantage. Then, motherhood. I can't think of one other role on this earth that requires *more* patience than that of a mother. And as soon as you master one type of patience, your fussy newborn who can't communicate what she needs turns into a mouthy toddler who demands the world, and you need to learn the new type of patience required for that next season of mothering. So yes, patience; mine definitely needed some fine-tuning.

2. **Functioning with less control.** Arguably, this was one of my stronger traits in my marketing career; maintaining *complete control* of my projects allowed me to accomplish my job efficiently, with attention to every important detail. But in my new role as a stay-at-home mom, those traits didn't translate well. In fact, they worked against me. After spending just a few weeks with my newborn, I quickly learned that complete

control was a thing of the past! Sure, you can *plan* to sleep for eight solid hours, run *all* of your errands in one day, keep a clean house, and cook three well-balanced meals a day, but then you come to terms with the real world of raising tiny humans, complete with sleep regressions, diaper blowouts, bouts of colic, and constraining nap schedules. It turns out you have very little control in the beginning. So yes, I needed to learn to function with much less control.

Toss what you must

Finally, I had two big items weighing me down as I made the transition from career woman to stay-at-home mom. I knew that in order to move forward in my new life, I'd have to lay these aspects of myself to rest (and may they RIP). I needed to *toss*:

1. **My need for status.** I took great pride in my job title with a Fortune 500 company. I stored a lot of my self-worth in that position (more on that later), and that made me feel important and accomplished in life. But there is no place or reason for status in motherhood. "Mom" is the most important role you'll ever have—it's a humbling and quietly powerful existence outside of the spotlight. Yes, my need for status had to go.

2. **Selfishness.** When you're an adult without children, you don't realize how selfish you really are. And then you have kids and you look back on your pre-baby life

that just reeks of selfishness and self-indulgence. All of that sleeping in on the weekends, going to a movie at 12 noon on a Sunday, staying out late and enjoying one too many margaritas with your girlfriends who you saw at least once a week, eating full meals, peeing alone—it was all just *so* selfish! Motherhood slapped the selflessness into me, complete with 3:30 a.m. wake-up calls, texting with old friends sporadically, eating Cheerios off of my toddler's plate and deeming that a meal, and peeing with a tiny human on my lap. Yes, selfishness had to go, too.

Draw a line

Comparing your old career life to life at home with your children is like comparing apples and oranges; they're just different. You're different in each of those roles. And if you continue living in the past and comparing your new role to your old role, you're not giving your new existence as a stay-at-home mom a fair chance to bring you happiness and fulfillment.

....

"I was surprised to find that the education and skills for managing projects and people I had didn't translate well to managing my home. Often I asked myself, how could I have managed a business and oversaw employees but I couldn't get a handle on running my own home?! I realized a home isn't something to manage at all; it's a haven for us to create uniquely for our families." —Amanda Ortega

....

As with all transitions in life, you're leaving some of yourself behind and awakening new parts of yourself as you progress forward. Its growth and new self-discovery disguised by the uncertainty of change. In order to embrace your new life as a stay-at-home mom, it's essential that you draw a clear line in the sand: letting go of your old career life and fully accepting your new role at home with your child/children.

If you find that you're straddling the line, with one foot still in your past career and one foot in your new role as a stay-at-home mom, now is the time to move both feet into the present and truly ground yourself in your new reality. You'll need this stability as you journey forward.

Exercise: Keep, Improve, Toss

Close your eyes and picture yourself at your old job. *What are you working on? What are you thinking about? What are your short-term and long-term goals? What's important to you in that season of your life? What kind of person are you?*

Use the following table to list what parts of your old career self that you want to keep, what you'd like to improve upon, and what you need to toss as you embrace this next chapter of your life. Use this transition period to:

1. Weed out any traits or ideals you may not have liked about yourself in your past career life or that may not translate well to your new role.

2. Improve upon characteristics that may need some special attention as you transition to a stay-at-home mom.

3. Hold on tight to the things that are so completely a
    part of you; they're non-negotiables as you journey
    into this new chapter.

Create a table with three columns. Write "Keep" at the
top of the first column, "Improve" at the top of the second
column, and "Toss" at the top of the third column. Then, list
all of the things you will keep, improve upon, or toss.

Reflect

Keep

Study your "Keep" column because these items are an
important part of you and will help you unlock your own
happiness as a stay-at-home mom. Each trait or characteris-
tic you wrote down in this column is a part of yourself that
you need to focus on as you transition from your old job to
life on the home front. These are keepsakes of yourself that
are probably the foundation of your makeup. Hold onto these
tight and make them a priority through your transition and
beyond. Without them you will likely slip into an existence
that is uncomfortable and, perhaps, unhappy. By keeping this
column front and center, you'll be able to fully create your
new life as a stay-at-home mom in a way that is true to you
and what you need in order to thrive.

Improve

Your responses in the "Improve" column are almost as
important as your "Keep" column because these are parts
of yourself that you have willingly acknowledged as needing

some work in order to be the best mom possible and to live a happy existence. Place these next to your "Keep" items in your soul and consciously seek circumstances, activities, and experiences that allow you to practice and fine-tune these aspects of yourself.

Toss

Nobody is perfect. We can all pinpoint parts of ourselves that we want to dispose of and try again. What was once important and helpful to us in our career lives may become utterly unimportant and useless to us as stay-at-home moms. Look at your "Toss" column and fully comprehend why you may need to lay certain aspects of yourself to rest in order to succeed in your new role as a mother. Then, let your soul settle into peace as you bid them farewell and begin down your new path with all the best parts of yourself in play.

Eulogy for my career self

We're gathered here today to mourn the loss of Kristin Helms, the marketing manager. We'll miss her well-controlled projects, decisiveness, and ability to meet her incentive bonuses every quarter, but we must lay her to rest in order for her to fully embrace her new identity as a stay-at-home mom.

Although we'll miss this version of Kristin, we know she'll embark on her new journey, keeping only the best parts of herself, continuously working on improving certain aspects of herself for her family, and shedding the dissatisfactory parts that have no place or importance in her new role as a stay-at-home mom.

Exercise: Eulogy for your career self

Now, write your own eulogy for your career self. Pack up everything you're taking with you—the best stuff and the stuff you'll work on along the way—and leave the rest behind. May it RIP.

Affirmations

- Today, I fully embrace my new role as a stay-at-home mom.
- Both of my feet are planted firmly here, in the now.
- I don't need to look to the past to see where I'm going.
- I'm living in the present and looking forward to the future.
- I bring the best parts of myself to my new role as a stay-at-home mom.
- My heart and soul feel light and happy as I clear anything negative holding me back.
- I'm ready to make my time at home count.

Chapter 3

New Beginnings:
Intentions, Goals, and Grace

*"There will come a time when you believe everything is finished.
That will be the beginning."*
—Louis L'Amour

I glance up from my seat on the couch, my eyes squinting to read the time on the microwave in the kitchen. 9:12 a.m. A little over two hours into my new role, my big decision, my new existence.

My daughter sleeps soundly on my chest, her three-month-old being relying quite entirely on me for support. The weight of that thought threatens to smash me. I rub her tiny back and take a deep breath. Today is my first Monday, after maternity leave, as a stay-at-home mom.

I walk carefully up the stairs to the nursery and gently place her into a cradle before heading to the bathroom. The gentle flick of the light switch is a surprising and welcomed sound in my new sea of silence.

I splash water on my face then open the medicine cabinet to retrieve my toothbrush, my thoughts conjuring my dear friend's stern advice: *Don't forget to take care of yourself.*

I vigorously start brushing while assessing my reflection. No makeup, although these bags under my eyes are begging for some concealer. No business suit, but these pajamas with breastmilk stains are making *quite* the statement. No meetings lined up for today, unless you count our mini Groundhog's Day routine—breastfeed, snuggle, sleep, repeat. No email notifications popping up on my phone—I know because I keep checking out of habit. I already feel forgotten.

This is me, 2.0—stripped of a job title, colleagues, hygiene— my carefully decorated resume, retired. It will take some time to get to know this person—the woman behind the suit, behind the ambition for success through career, behind 16 years of employment and building equity in myself.

It's not lost on me that other moms on the flip side of this coin are looking into the mirror, holding back tears as they get ready to leave their babies asleep in cradles while returning back to their jobs. The magnitude of the decision is startling: It takes courage to leave. It takes courage to stay.

Counseling advice
"In the Woody Allen movie Annie Hall, *Allen's character says to his girlfriend (Annie Hall, played by Diane Keaton) 'A relationship, I think, is like a shark…it has*

to constantly move forward or it dies.' I don't know if this is true about sharks, but I feel it is true to our sense of self, self-worth, and fulfillment in our lives. While you were working outside of the home, growth in your career was almost fundamental: What new skills can I learn and/or improve upon, what are my strengths, how do I show up? This is also exactly true to your new role as stay-at-home mom. You are now leaning into your life in the same way while learning completely different skills. Growth and change can be exhilarating and dynamic and fun. Growth and change can also be scary and uncomfortable and may even evoke doubt and uncertainty. It's all in the same package. Remember who you are, ground yourself in this knowledge, take a deep breath, and remember a quote by Mandy Hale: 'It's okay to be scared. Being scared means you're about to do something really, really brave.'" —Karen Simms, mental health counselor

Starting off on the right foot

As with all great adventures, the beginning is a little scary. Leaving a well-established career and heading blindly into a new existence without any sort of pre-existing structure takes courage. While you previously relied on the stability and clear-cut tasks and goals that your past career life provided, you'll need to learn how to rely on yourself to offer the same sense of stability, routine, and goal-setting for your new role as a stay-at-home mom. There are no existing meetings, career guidance, big-picture goals, or to-do lists offered to you on your first Monday as a stay-at-home mom. It's up to you to design this role however you see fit.

....

"Going to work is predictable. I had a set schedule, a job description of tasks that needed to be accomplished, and a time frame in which to do them. Becoming a stay-at-home mom meant I dictated everything (well, besides the obvious fact that the baby was really in command), I was the one deciding the importance of the tasks for the day, whether or not I had to get dressed or even leave the house; I only had myself to report to throughout the day. It was liberating and thrilling and terrifying to find myself with that much power." —Beth Robinson

....

In a way, it's like starting your own business; you'll need to lay a strong foundation based on your core values, build a framework through a solid mission statement, and then make it all come to life with a driving purpose.

Let the weight of this sink into your being: You have all the power now. No one is looking over your shoulder to make sure you're producing quality work, there's no HR department helping direct and advance your skills, there are no quarterly reviews to deliver critique, praise, rewards, and validation. It's just you and your precious tiny human(s). Your sole job is to guide souls, shape minds, and lead by example, 24 hours a day, seven days a week.

So how will you make your time at home count? How will you design a life full of happiness for your family and fulfillment for yourself? In order to start off on the right foot, it's important to identify intentions and goals for your time at home.

Setting intentions for your time at home

From your very first Monday as a stay-at-home mom, it's important to set mindful intentions for you and your family. Think of your intentions as part of a mission statement. What is your overall mission as a stay-at-home mom? Do you wish to raise grounded humans who know right from wrong? Do you want to raise your child/children within a certain faith? Do you want to instill gratitude and kindness above all? Do you want to bring up the next leaders of tomorrow?

Think about why you chose to stay home in the first place (perhaps revisiting your exercises from Chapter 1) and then think about your overall mission as a foundation for your time at home. By setting intentions from the start, you'll give yourself a North Star to guide you as you blaze your unique journey through motherhood.

"The biggest surprise to me was how relentless staying at home feels. Even though work wasn't easy or a break, per se, the separation from my kids allowed me to bring more of myself to our relationship when we were together. Staying home, it's impossible to be on for them all the time." —Lorren Lemmons

When you start to get lost in the day-to-day hustle as a stay-at-home mom—when the days become long, the tasks of caring for babies and toddlers stretch you to your limit, and when the endless chores become mundane—look to your North Star, these intentions you set at the beginning of your journey, for guidance. Recenter yourself on this big picture and find peace in knowing everything you do, day in and day out, has a purpose—a big, beautiful purpose. While you're in the thick of it, your purpose may become blurry and it may become hard to define the difference you're truly making in your children's lives. Remind yourself to step back from the details of the daily grind, when you need encouragement the most, and take another look at the big picture you've created through your mission statement and the intentions you've set. Know that everything you're doing counts.

Exercise: Mission and intentions

1. Write down a one or two sentence mission statement for your time as a stay-at-home mom. Remember to think about the big picture of why you chose this role in the first place.

2. Considering your mission statement, list five intentions you wish to accomplish during your time at home.

Example

My mission statement + 5 big intentions

Mission Statement: I want to lead and support my daughter and my son so they have the right tools to navigate the world with kindness and strength.

Five big-picture intentions I want to accomplish during my time at home:

1. *Teaching kindness.*
2. *Teaching respect.*
3. *Teaching gratitude.*
4. *Fostering strength and independence.*
5. *Instilling a moral compass.*

Setting mindful goals

Now that we've successfully laid the foundation for our time at home, through our big-picture intentions, we'll also need to outline the ways in which we will fulfill those intentions.

As a past career woman, you're probably familiar with goals. In the workforce, perhaps goals existed as tangible rewards for meeting or exceeding expectations, obtaining stellar customer satisfaction ratings, or receiving promotions.

In motherhood, the obvious goal is to raise good human beings, but the pathways to getting there are different for every mother. By mindfully setting small goals to accomplish daily, weekly, monthly, and yearly, you will help build a clear path to raising your children based on your values and staying true to your overall intentions for your time as a stay-at-home mom.

Although each goal by itself may seem minute in the grand scheme of parenting, together they'll establish a well-crafted blueprint, helping shape your children and define your unique mission as a stay-at-home mom.

Exercise: Craft your blueprint

Create your own blueprint for your family. A large part of creating your goals will depend on your child's/children's age(s), so it's a good idea to update your goals as your children grow and need different things from you. List:

- Your daily goals.
- Your weekly goals.
- Your monthly goals.
- Your yearly goals.

Example

Daily Goals

Practice "please" and "thank you."

Work on talking through tantrums to get to the root of the issue.

Answer all the "but why?" questions to the best of my knowledge.

Silly/wild/dancing time together.

Quiet/reading time together.

Encourage independent play.

Outdoor time together for some fresh air and vitamin D.

Stick to a nap time and bed time routine.

Weekly Goals

Arrange at least three family dinners with all members present around the same table.

Go on at least two adventures outside of the house (park, library, beach, walk, kids museum, zoo, and so on).

Organize at least two different art projects to try.

Monthly Goals

Plan a new experience (visit a farm, fly a kite, learn how to scooter).

Teach and reward simple chores around the house.

Yearly Goals

Plan at least one family vacation.

Put together a scrapbook of the year.

Volunteer our time (donate old clothes, pack lunches for homeless shelters, and so on).

Discuss and reflect on what we loved best about the past year and brainstorm goals for the year ahead.

Practicing grace

While we're busy planning our intentions and goals for our time as stay-at-home moms, we can't forget the living, breathing, adorable little curveballs: our children. Raising babies/toddlers/kids doesn't always fit into a perfectly crafted blueprint. Messes are made, tears are shed, and some days it's impossible to get out of the house in one piece, let alone achieve any pre-determined goals.

....

*"I was amazed at how hard it was and how my day filled up with just basic baby care. I could barely get dinner made." —*Lisa Druxman
....

This season of life is hard, and that's true for all mothers, whether you're a stay-at-home mom, working mom, or mompreneur. Just remember: The goals are meant to help you keep a place of center within the chaos and uncertainty of motherhood. You won't always be able to check everything off of your to-do list, keep a clean house, or prepare Pinterest-worthy meals. Use your outlined goals purely as guidance along your parenting journey but also leave room for the unexpected.

Above all, allow yourself grace throughout motherhood. As mothers it's hard to see your colicky baby who won't stop crying, your toddler who is having a meltdown in aisle five at Target, or your child who won't share his sand toys at the park. Our immediate reaction is always to place blame on ourselves: *This is my fault. What am I doing wrong?* And that's not fair. There is no such thing as the perfect parent or the perfect child. Crying, meltdowns, and bad behavior are par for the course of raising tiny humans. There are big emotions in little bodies and a steep learning curve for both mother and child. It's our job as moms to search for the teachable moments, do our best to instill our values in our children along the way, and allow ourselves grace through it all.

Controlling thoughts and reactions

While navigating the open seas of motherhood and practicing grace, it's helpful to acknowledge the things you know are out of your control so you don't feel like a failure when they don't go as planned.

You cannot control how much sleep you'll get every night while your children are babies or even toddlers. You can will them to sleep through the night, pray, and read baby sleep articles written by "experts" until you go cross-eyed, but the actual hours of sleep you'll receive each night are out of your control.

Routines may also be out of your control in the early child-rearing years. You will probably try to set some sort of daily routine, but children will get sick, developmental leaps will shake the system, daylight savings time happens twice a year throwing everything off kilter, and you'll constantly be revising the "plan."

Luckily, you'll be able to control two big things. You'll be able to control your thoughts and, with practice, your reactions. You can choose to wake up every day grateful or ungrateful, happy or mad, motivated or lazy. You have power over your internal thoughts; practice controlling them in a way that fosters happiness and grace.

When your toddler is throwing a fit in the grocery store, you can teach yourself how to count to three in your head, very slowly, before mindfully reacting. You can take control of a situation that is out of your control, by harnessing your thoughts and reactions.

Of course this will all take time and practice. And through it all, find peace in knowing you're not alone. You're not the only mother who feels like she's reached her limit sometimes. You're not the only mother who feels like she doesn't know what she's doing most of the time. Motherhood takes strength, patience, and persistence. Make sure your tank is full of grace as you navigate this season.

Exercise: Controlling the uncontrollable

Write down three things you know you can control every day. Write down three things you know you cannot control every day.

By acknowledging all of the things out of your control, you will rid yourself of the disappointment that stems from unmet expectations. Conversely, becoming mindfully aware of the things you can control will empower you to manage your thoughts, emotions, and actions through unexpected circumstances. Identifying and internalizing the uncontrollable and controllable gives you a new sense of power and a happier existence as a stay-at-home mom.

Affirmations

- I begin my journey as a stay-at-home mom focused and prepared.
- My role as a stay-at-home mom is momentous.
- Everything I do as a stay-at-home mom helps shape my child/children into the person/people he/she/they will become one day.
- I know my intentions and mission for my time at home with my child/children.

- I know what I want to accomplish daily, weekly, monthly, yearly for my family.
- I give myself grace throughout motherhood.
- I know I can't control everything.
- I possess the power to control my thoughts and reactions in this season of life.
- I am proud of myself for providing a strong foundation for my family.

Section 2:
Navigating Through the Transition

Chapter 4

Changes in Relationships With Your Partner, Friends, and Family

"Any change, even a change for the better, is always accompanied by drawbacks and discomforts."
—Arnold Bennett

"But enough about my day, how was yours?" my husband asked as we picked up the scattered toys in the playroom after putting our daughter to bed.

"It was good! Miss B was making this really cute snoot face while she was eating a banana this morning. And then we went for a walk around the block. She took some great naps today." I tried to recall any interesting details or complex thoughts— I had nothing. Gone were the days of sharing work projects, office politics, and business strategies with each other after grinding all day at the office. My daily adult interactions now included our mailman and a couple neighbors. My biggest decision involved whether or not to defrost the chicken or the beef for dinner. I had officially become uninteresting.

I noticed this awkward conversation happening, not only with my husband, but also with old work friends and even some of my extended family members. I didn't really have much to talk about outside of baby sleep schedules and child developmental brags. I could actually feel the discomfort in these conversations; they didn't know what to ask me, and I didn't know what to offer.

Besides conversations, our life structure had changed, too. Pre-baby times meant weekends sleeping in and strolling over to brunch at a non-kid-friendly establishment around noon. It meant sporadic date nights without early end-times and stops at the ATM on the way home to get enough cash for the babysitter. It meant meeting up for drinks with friends on a whim. It meant leisurely weekend road trips or international vacations, sans car seats, iPads stocked with *Daniel Tiger* episodes, and packing up the entire house. It meant quick solo trips to the grocery store sans toddler meltdowns, in and out in 10 minutes flat. It meant being selfish and free, together.

Then we became parents. The comfortable, familiar life we had built together suddenly became complicated and full of earth-shattering decisions. Like, do we really need a baby wipe warmer? How do you use this contraption called a NoseFrida? Should we swaddle or use a sleep sack? What's the best cream to use for diaper rashes? Is it just gas or is it colic? Is this normal or should we call the pediatrician? So many questions warranted undivided attention.

Our world turned from focusing on each other and ourselves to shifting 100 percent of our attention to our new baby. I remember, in those early days as a new mom, when my husband and I were both on maternity and paternity leave, and our daughter was finally asleep at the end of the day, I'd look up at my husband and say, "I feel like I haven't seen you all day." Of course, that was an odd thing to say because he was right next to me through it all as we intensely navigated nursing positions, carefully counted hours between feedings, strategically burped the baby, bathed the baby, and alternated diaper-changing duties. The attention that our new precious little babe demanded from us left little room to provide attention toward one another; which was a complete 180 in our relationship.

But kids also change your being in the most magnificent ways. Looking back at my pre-baby life, full of freedom and spontaneity, I still would trade any and all of it for my precious babies. Of course, I sometimes miss my old life— especially on the more trying days. But, my existence has taken on so much more meaning. Some days, I think my heart might just burst into a million pieces with the overflowing love found in our daily lives. For weaved throughout the chaos and the worry and the undivided attention lives this strand of sheer and utter happiness. And I can't imagine life without this magic.

Relationship with your partner

You and your partner have probably experienced many life changes together through the course of your relationship:

new jobs, new homes, deaths in the family, and the addition of new family members. As with all big life changes, it's important to let the new normal settle and then tweak your relationship as needed to support your new normal.

Becoming parents is momentous. You can prepare for it down to the last neatly folded onesie, yet somehow when baby arrives, you end up feeling ill prepared. Leaving your job to become a stay-at-home mom while your partner steps into the role as sole financial provider for your family, only add more uncertainty and more change.

Pay attention to each other during the transition. You'll need to learn what each other needs in order to thrive as you both find your footing in your new roles. It may take some time, but give each other lots of grace, understanding, and encouragement and you'll find your rhythm, together.

Supporting each other in your new roles

While my husband and I always supported each other through work and our careers, we had to learn how to support each other through parenting—me now as a stay-at-home mom, and him as the sole financial supporter of our family. This took time and open lines of communication throughout the transition. Mostly, I needed to learn what he needed in order to succeed in his new role, and he needed to learn what I needed to succeed in mine.

Although I would never fully understand what it felt like for him to be the sole provider for his family and the stress and pressure that weighed upon him, we tried to communicate and identify ways I could support him. For us, this included me taking on more of our once-shared responsibilities at home—grocery shopping and meal prep, cleaning the house, doing the laundry, and buying anything he might need while I was out running errands. However he needed help in order to keep his focus on bringing home a paycheck for our family, I would aid him in those responsibilities.

Conversely, my husband would never understand what it felt like for me to be the sole caretaker of our baby—and more recently, two toddlers—and the stress and self-sacrifice that weighed upon me throughout my days. Again, we kept our lines of communication open, discussing the hardships that I was battling along my new journey. He quickly realized that it was important for me to hear affirmations of value from him—the affirmations that I was now missing by not bringing home a paycheck. Although it's such a small gesture for a partner to tell you how much value and worth you bring to the family, hearing those words, especially on the hard days, makes all the difference. When adult interactions are slim, sometimes it's just nice to feel seen.

Mano a mano

Probably one of the most important ways to keep open lines of communication with your partner and truly grow together through the transition is to arrange alone time together. The slippery slope of just coexisting is easy to fall into while caring for tiny humans.

Although fancy date nights complete with a babysitter are nice, time together can also mean simply putting your phones down and talking over a homemade dinner that you prepared together after the baby is asleep. Perhaps you arrange phone-free dinners, at the dinner table, at least twice a week.

It's also important to get out of the house together. You will recharge both of your souls and strengthen your connection within this new chapter of your lives by experiencing little pieces of old pastimes—revisiting your favorite restaurants pre-kids, challenging each other to a game of mini-golf like you did on your first date, or simply holding hands in a movie theater while catching the newest blockbuster.

My husband and I also found it important to escape completely from our everyday lives, even for just 24 hours. We enlisted our parents or my sisters to watch the kids while we indulged in a simple staycation at a local hotel with an amazing pool and great spa, or road-tripped to a nearby city robust with new adventures. As the kids grew older, we felt more and more comfortable leaving them with family for an entire weekend or more, and traveling a little further from home base. Whether you can escape for just 24 hours or a few days, planning trips is an amazing way to reconnect without the stresses of everyday life.

Standing united

As new parents, you've probably already experienced the overwhelming amount of advice and well-intentioned tips you receive from friends and family members. Suddenly, everyone is an expert and wants to be involved in the child-rearing. Although it's great to have support from loved ones, it can also lead to stress on your relationship with your partner.

It's important for you and your partner to together identify your unique core values, discuss and decide upon large decisions as they relate to your child/children, and most importantly, stand united when explaining and defending those values and decisions to outside influences. Remembering you're a team in life, and throughout this season of raising tiny humans, is paramount as you parent together.

Topics of interest

Since my husband and I had previously related a great deal through working full-time jobs and helping each other navigate careers, it was important for us to find new ways to correlate when I became a stay-at-home mom. Obviously, our new baby was a big way for us to connect as new parents—caring for and loving our precious little girl who we had brought into this world, together. But beyond updating my husband about all of the cute (or not-so-cute) things that happened to my daughter and I throughout our days, I began searching for additional topics of interest.

I began using my daughter's nap times to learn about new interesting topics. Not only so I could have something beyond diaper duties to discuss, but also because it helped exercise my brain throughout the day. I made a list of 20 new topics I wanted to learn more about, and instead of mindlessly scrolling through Facebook or Instagram for the umpteenth time, I dedicated my down time to researching new topics.

It's fascinating how much you can learn about a topic from simple scrolls and clicks on your iPhone. Suddenly, I felt like I had a whole new toolkit full of conversation starters and knowledge ready to offer to any and all who would listen. Learning about new topics and ideas also boosted my self-esteem and replaced my feelings of not using enough brain-power throughout the day with feelings of empowerment and knowledge—homeschooling for the stay-at-home mom, if you will.

Exercise: Conversation bits

List 20 topics or ideas you're interested in learning more about (think: cooking, foreign language, politics, science, art, child development, history, nutrition, exercise, law, foreign affairs, botany, spirituality, and so on).

Dedicate your down time to learning more about one to two topics on your list each week.

Relationships with your friends and family

As the saying goes, "Your vibe attracts your tribe." You've probably made great friendships and connections through your past job and throughout your professional career. Not to mention, your extended family members probably associate you with your old job or your industry of expertise. So, what happens when your vibe changes? Does your tribe need to change, too? Or can your tribe change with you?

Getting to know the new you

I've found that finding new friends who are experiencing the same joys and hardships of motherhood as you are is a huge key to happiness in your new role (more on this in Chapter 7). But, equally important, is finding a way to transition your old relationships with extended family members and close friends into your new life as a stay-at-home mom.

At first, it may be difficult. You're transitioning to a stay-at-home mom and redefining yourself and your life. Your friends and family will need to get to know the new you and learn how to connect and support you in your new role.

Of course, you're still *you*, but you'll also be different. The once energetic, willing to drop everything and meet up for dinner or talk on the phone for an hour friend/sister/daughter is now terribly sleep deprived, has to preschedule any sort of meet-up weeks (maybe months) in advance, and only communicates through text messages.

Enlightening your old friends and family members about how your life is changing and sharing the hardships and triumphs that you may be experiencing in your new role as a stay-at-home mom will help your loved ones understand your new life. Open communication will also allow your relationships to grow and evolve through the change.

It's also important to physically invite your friends and family into your new life so they can see you in your new capacity. Invite old friends over for family dinners or encourage them to join you on family outings. Seeing you in your new role as Mom will allow them to find ways to connect with you on a new level.

Reserving time to reconnect with old friends and family members, without the kids in tow, is also important. Precious new additions to families are always the focal point at get-togethers or parties. It's important to find time to reconnect with your loved ones alone, giving you the chance to catch up, have deeper conversations, and each other's undivided attention.

Exercise: Carving out time

List all of your loved ones: your partner, old friends, and family members.

Brainstorm and write down ways to carve out time for each of them. For example: Schedule a babysitter once a month and plan a date night with my husband; invite my sister to coffee on Sunday morning when my husband can watch the baby, which allows my sister and I to catch up just the two of us; invite an old friend to the zoo with my kids and me on Saturday so she can connect with me and really see me within my new role as a mom.

Counseling advice
"This chapter truly addresses the notion of intimacy with the people in our lives; it looks at the connections we have made and notices the strengths of those connections and perhaps the areas that need more attention

in order to weather the life change and transition of having a child and choosing to stay home. There are various ways that we show up and create intimate connections: With emotional intimacy, we show vulnerability, we share our deepest thoughts, worries, hopes, dreams, and we speak from a deeper place inside ourselves. With mental intimacy, we align, validate, create strong bonds of kinship, and feel an integral part of a 'tribe.'

When making this considerable change in your lives, you may notice how you may have relied on reporting about your day as a main way of connecting. This life change gives you the opportunity to strengthen intimate conversations, and to transcend talking about events to talking about ideas and feelings, including your thoughts and feelings about the events of your day, such as how your heart melted with love when 'Miss B was making this really cute snoot face while she was eating a banana.' Now we are talking about our hearts and love and, voila, intimacy. Notice your self-talk during this transition and have grace for yourself as you shift your self-identity. You will have many roles in your life, often all at the same time. Take a deep breath, ground yourself in remembering your core self: a woman of heart, love, joy, intention, and earnestness." —Karen Simms, mental health counselor

Affirmations

- Relationships that can evolve throughout life are the ones worth keeping.
- Supporting my partner in his/her new role strengthens our relationship.
- Communicating my needs to my partner through this transition strengthens our relationship.
- Relationships with my loved ones are an important part of my past, present, and future.
- I am an interesting person with so much to offer.

Chapter 5

Molding the Mundanity and Chaos Into Lessons, Love, and Life

"The power of finding beauty in the humblest of things makes home happy and life lovely."
—Louisa May Alcott

"Be careful honey, this is really hot," my voice teetered on-edge and it was only 8:15 a.m. My 2-year-old daughter clung to my side like a monkey, insisting on helping scramble the eggs while my 10-month-old son tried to climb up my leg with his sharp little nails digging into my calves, a painful reminder that I needed to cut those little dinosaur claws. All I wanted was five minutes and two free hands so I could put breakfast on the table.

"Bye guys, have a good day," my husband said as he kissed us and headed out the door to work.

After struggling to get my son in his high chair, my daughter in her booster seat, and breakfast in front of them, my phone dinged with a new text message. It was from my husband, a photo he had taken of us on his way out the door—during our egg-scrambling fiasco and what I had mentally chalked up as a chaotic morning scene. But studying the photo, all I saw was love. The stress of the moment was somehow swallowed by the obvious love—my daughter clinging to my left hip with her head resting on my shoulder and my son who can't go two minutes without touching Mama as he reached up for me—it was all love.

In that moment, studying the photo, I realized: This is what motherhood is. It's taking the chaos and molding it into love, finding the balance between trying to get things done and trying to savor the little moments. And it's hard and it's messy, but it's fueled by love. And my tank is full.

Acknowledging the hard stuff

Mamas, here's the real, stripped-down, strikingly honest truth: This season of life is tough. Being a stay-at-home mom is tough. I was caught off-guard on just how difficult it was to take on a role that demanded my complete attention 24 hours a day, 7 days a week.

"I am more exhausted on a daily basis than I ever was as a working mom." —Michelle Nelson

Let's acknowledge all the hardships of being a stay-at-home mom and get these words off our chests and out into the open: mundane, sacrificial, hard work, selfless, chaotic, boring, lackluster, patience-testing, limit-pushing, physically taxing, tiring, overwhelming, lonely. Feel free to add additional words—anything negative you might be feeling about your new role.

....

"I never expected the degree of stress and responsibility I'd experience being a stay-at-home mom. One will not stress or worry over a typo or incorrectly prepared report the way they will worry about their child choking on food, falling off the couch, making sure their child is learning what they are supposed to know for their particular age bracket. Taking care of a person is far more taxing than taking care of paperwork, needs of management, and disgruntled clients." —Marisa Svalstedt

....

Just reading these words is therapeutic. (I know writing them down felt really good for me, too!) As stay-at-home moms we instinctually feel guilty when we're not happy or enjoying every second with our children at home. Maybe it's because we feel like we don't deserve to have this role if we're not enjoying it 100 percent of the time. That's just absurd. We are human, and these adversities, par for the stay-at-home mom course, are not for the faint of heart. These are incredibly trying realities we're faced with daily. It's important to acknowledge them so we don't expect a rose-colored life full of only good moments, at home raising children. And most importantly, let's acknowledge them here and now so we don't feel guilty when they pop up through the course of our journey as stay-at-home moms.

> *"The feelings of loneliness, unrealistic expectations, and overwhelming guilt is what surprised me most about being a stay-at-home mom. I expected never-ending play dates, endless amounts of personal creativity, and an immaculate home. Basically, the perfect life with the Facebook page to prove it and copious amounts of energy to do it all."* —Rachel Rainforth

Now that we've acknowledged and brought forth our biggest hardships we're faced with in our new role, let's focus on what tools we have to combat these obstacles and unveil a more fulfilling life as a stay-at-home mom.

Uncovering the good stuff

As I write this book, my kiddos are 1 and 3 years old. Most of our days are chaos. I referee fights, kiss boo-boos, prepare meals and snacks that mostly go uneaten or are later swept up from the floor, and I count to three in my head over and over, grasping for patience though it all. I try to teach lessons along the way, explain how things work, answer questions, and reward empathy. I'm thoughtfully surviving—reminding myself to take steps back from the daily grit so I can look at the big picture and make sure I'm not screwing it all up. I know I'll look back on the photos I take and the words I write, and I'll miss this chaos. I'll miss this all-consuming season of motherhood. But today, I'll focus on allowing myself grace—acknowledging the magic of it all, accepting the imperfections, and soaking in the love.

• • • • • • • •

It's up to us to shape our outlook, mold our days, and lead our families' lives into meaningful existences. Never underestimate the power of positive thoughts. We can choose to mentally break down along with our messy houses, scattered toys, and mischievous toddlers. Or, we can remind ourselves to see past the chaos: The house is messy and the toys are scattered because I was too busy playing "house" with my 2-year-old and I didn't have time to clean—my time together with her was more important in that moment. And when she told me "I love you to the moon" and kissed me on the forehead and tucked me into my make-believe "bed" (just as I recite the same phrase while tucking her into her bed every night), my heart skipped a beat, because I'm really showing her how to love and be loved. I realize she is a reflection of me and the examples I'm setting.

And my 1-year-old is Mr. Mischievous because he is just so curious about life that he can't help but touch and experience everything. He's growing up right before my eyes, learning how the world works, and I get to witness every second of it and help guide him through these fundamental years. I get to see the world anew through his curious eyes.

There is magic in the mess, if you're willing to look for it.

Exercise: Finding magic

Write down the three most trying moments you experienced in the last week. Next to each, write down the hidden magic you can find when you look a little closer.

Example

Trying moment: My 6-month-old is going through a sleep regression and won't go back to sleep unless I rock her for 30 minutes in the middle of the night.

Hidden magic: I have the power to help my daughter get back to sleep, and my very presence puts her at peace and makes her feel safe. Now, that is magic!

Reset buttons

Tantrums, teething, and all, we were a tornado trapped inside of a SUV heading home from some errands. Desperate for a reset button, I made an impulse decision (gasp!) to stop at the beach. No towels, no toys, no change of clothes, no snacks. Just us. Take us as we are, imperfections and all! And while our feet scampered across wet sand and the salt air filled our lungs, a beautiful thing happened: The tear-stained cheeks turned to smiles and laughter, the fighting over "things" turned into playing make-believe together illuminated by the sunset, and the sour moods turned to pure joy. The sandy car seats and late dinnertime that followed were well worth that magic.

· · · · · · · ·

You will get stuck in some of the privations of being a stay-at-home mom—we all do. Some days, your toddler will wake up in a mood and you'll be running on just a few hours of sleep because the baby was up all night teething, and you'll just know that it's going to be one of those days.

....

"It's a constant battle against entropy. I do the same things over and over because they constantly are undone by my children." —Jess Hernandez

....

When times get tough, and you're having trouble uncovering the good stuff, try resetting the course of your day. A simple recourse can do wonders for jump-starting yourself out of a funk.

Toolkit: Suggestions to reset your day

Consider some of the following suggestions to help reset your more trying days:

- Take a walk. Packing your child/children into the stroller and going for a walk allows you a small break, while getting your blood and endorphins flowing.

- Go for a drive. Having your children fastened securely in their car seats while you drive around and experience a change of scenery is sometimes just the break you need.

- Play some fun music and turn it up really loud. When in doubt, just dance.

- Start talking with an accent. Sometimes your day just needs a light-hearted touch to remind you not to take life too seriously. Your kids will likely get a kick out of this, too.

- Tell your kiddos to gather around like you're at a campfire, and tell them a make-believe or fairytale story.

- Go to a body of water (ocean, lake, pond). Sometimes our deepest thoughts and greatest revelations are made where land meets water.

- Turn chores into a game. Who can pick up all the toys the fastest? Who can make their bed the best?

- Get out of your bubble. We all live in some sort of bubble, otherwise known as our immediate comfort zone/neighborhood. Purposely pack up your kiddos and escape the familiar—go and experience something new, even if you have to drive 30-minutes or more to get there. (#worthit.)

- Call another mom and combine the chaos. Having someone to vent to, like another mother who knows exactly what you're going through, while your children entertain each other, kills two birds with one stone.

- Put your child/children in the bath. There's no set rule that says bath times are only meant for the end of each day. Sometimes, simple fun in the tub is the perfect change of course and gives you a foot-up on the impending bedtime routine.

- Facetime with a relative or a friend: Reaching the outside world while you feel stuck inside of your own can revive your spirit. Plus, I haven't met a toddler who doesn't love a good Facetime session.

- Go to your local nursery or grocery store and buy yourself some fresh flowers. You deserve it.

- Work out. Put on an exercise video at home and complete the moves with your kiddos or head to a gym that offers two-hours of free childcare.

- Plan an impromptu date night. Call your sitter and see if he's/she's available on short notice, and then plan something fun for you and your partner for later that night. The spontaneity of it all and giving yourself something to look forward to in your immediate future will work wonders.

- Break out the art supply container, either for you to create something crafty while your baby naps, or for your toddler to re-channel her attention.

. . . .

Counseling advice

"I love this chapter's intentionality and how it turns around perspectives. It asks, 'Can I see this moment in a different light?' and 'Can I be the author of the next moment?' But also, before you can get there, you need

*to name, without shame, some of the harder emotions
you may be feeling: frustration, boredom, irritation,
shame. Especially shame. Shame comes hand-in-hand
with our 'shoulds' and 'should nots.' Then comes guilt,
which is often the tried-and-true partner of shame.
With grace and self-compassion, try to understand
the source of these feelings. Is it an old story rearing
its head? Is it the notion that motherhood is blissful
and 'if I am not feeling blissful always does that mean
I am a bad mom/not doing this right/fill in the fear
you're feeling here?' During these moments in particular, give yourself the love, softness, and understanding
that you give your child when he or she is scared, hurt,
or concerned. This you have within you in abundance
and the more you use it, the more it grows.
To use Kristin's word, it's 'magical.' Regarding the idea
of '[let's] get these words off our chests': Externalizing
our feelings, especially the harder, darker ones, gives
us not only space to breath, but something to work
with. Now, you can have a 'relationship' with your
feelings. They are no longer stuck in your head or
heart, but out there as a separate entity that you can
understand in a deeper way. Through journaling or
art, externalizing our feelings is a healing way to get
a new perspective, find self-compassion, and have
loving opportunities to see the possible areas that
may need more guidance toward change."* —Karen
Simms, mental health counselor

Affirmations

- This all-consuming season of motherhood is tough, but I am strong.
- I have the power to uncover the magic found in our everyday mess.
- I have the power to reset bad days.
- There is beauty in the mess.
- Motherhood is molding the hardships into lessons, love, and life.
- I fuel myself with grace through the more trying days as a stay-at-home mom.
- I am thankful for my time at home with my baby/ babies.
- I am creating a beautiful life for my family.
- My job as a stay-at-home mom is hard, important, and beautiful.

Chapter 6

The Modern-Day Stay-at-Home Mom: Redefining the Role

"Set wide the window. Let me drink the day."
—Edith Wharton

During my first few months in my new role, I tried to emulate what I had seen in the media about being a "successful" stay-at-home mom. I devoted my entire attention to cleaning, cooking, and, obviously, caring for my precious babe. I kept an immaculate house, and I had dinner waiting on the table when my husband got home from work. I was Mrs. 1950s Housewife in the flesh. *Wasn't this what life as a stay-at-home mother looked like?* And if it did, why did it feel so uncomfortable?

I found that as a modern-day woman, I didn't fit the mold of the traditional stay-at-home mom. While domestic responsibilities still needed to be a part of my new role,

I began looking for ways to redefine this new path, on my own terms. From this realization came the courage to deprioritize the "expected" domestic routine and responsibilities and prioritize: raising good humans; venturing out of the house; nurturing my own body, mind, and soul; and empowering myself to resurrect old passions and turn those into a hobby, and eventually, a side business. Just because I was a stay-at-home mom didn't mean I was contractually obligated to stay home every day and iron my husband's underwear. There was a whole big wide world out there, and I suddenly gained the courage to go and explore it, with my precious kiddos! There were also depths of my soul and being that I hadn't tapped into in quite some time, and I felt inspired to uncover what was beneath the surface.

Redefining the role of a stay-at-home mom

While we may want to buck the system entirely and decide not to do laundry or cook meals, all in the name of modern stay-at-home mothering, that's not realistic. You will still need to carve out some time for managing your household. My battle cry is simply this: The role of a stay-at-home mom does not stop at domestic duties. You can make this existence so much more. The key is finding balance between your responsibilities at home and activities that will catapult your new existence into a whole new realm of possibility— *where self-esteem, self-worth, and happiness live.*

Some women may find happiness and fulfillment in washing dishes and ironing clothes, but I am not one of them. I do these things because they need to be done, but that's not where I'm going to base my fulfillment. No. I'm going to base my fulfillment in raising good humans, exercising my creativity, and exploring the world anew, through my children's eyes.

Consider creating more balance and fulfillment within your role by investing more time in the following ideas.

Raising good humans

This was probably one of the top reasons you left your career and stayed home in the first place, and may be a given, but I'd like to put it front and center. There is so much fulfillment in raising good humans. You can actually see when your lessons, nurturing, and love are mirrored back to you through your children—it's probably one of the best feelings in the world. Let this act as a reminder that the dishes can wait, the laundry will never end, but a child has an expiration date. Because babies grow into toddlers and toddlers turn into kids, and kids become teenagers and teenagers outgrow the house and are suddenly adulting on their own. Our time at home with our kids is fleeting and they need us for guidance *right now*. Never underestimate how much power and influence you have on this world; after all, the next generation is looking up at you, Mama. Let's make our time at home count.

Exploring

I remember the first day I was home alone with my precious new baby, after family had retreated back to their own lives and my husband returned back to work. I was terrified to leave the house. What if something happened that I couldn't handle by myself? What if she wouldn't stop crying? What if she had a massive poop blowout and I forgot to pack wipes? I felt ill-equipped to battle the outside world with a newborn in tow—I had only been a mom for 14 days! Then, I happened upon a website for new moms called RookieMoms.com. The name alone hooked me because I was obviously very "rookie" at this whole mom thing. Rookie Moms listed 52 weekly challenges that encouraged new moms to get out of the house with a baby. Not suggestions, *challenges*! Never one to back down from a good challenge, I was intrigued. It was just the sort of motivation I needed to reenter the outside world with my baby. As I began planning and experiencing new excursions with my baby, my confidence as a mother grew. I felt more connected to the world outside of my home, and I made some incredible memories with my daughter through those early motherhood months—a special time as we both learned how to navigate the world, together.

Toolkit: Outing suggestions

Get out of the house and explore the world with your kiddos in tow. Consider visiting:

- Coffee shops
- Museums
- A body of water
- Hiking trails

- Library story times
- Open gyms at gymnastics centers
- Barnes & Noble story times
- Pet stores
- Petting zoos
- Local pools/splash pads
- Music/sign-language/Gymboree classes (free trial classes are usually available)
- Malls
- Seasonal outings (fairs, holiday lights, the circus coming to town, exhibits, and so on)
- The zoo
- Picnics
- Mommy and me fitness classes (think: mommy and me yoga, barre and baby classes, or Fit4Mom classes)
- Go for a bike ride (purchase a kid's bike seat to put on the back or front of you own bike)
- Berry picking fields
- A local farm
- The farmer's market
- A butterfly farm
- Old town
- Downtown
- Sports games
- Train or trolley rides around your city

Exercise: Tourist mom

Research two new outings in your area each week and get out and explore with your child/children in tow.

Document each experience with photos and maybe even a journal entry so you can look back on those precious early motherhood moments with your adorable sidekick for years to come.

Volunteering

A great way to fill your free time with more meaning and purpose is by volunteering with an organization that resonates with you and your values. You may wish to find volunteer work that is conducive to bringing your baby with you during the week, or you may decide to dedicate an evening or one of your weekend mornings, when your partner is home to take over childcare responsibilities. The best form of fulfillment often comes from giving rather than receiving. Connecting with your local community and providing value and aid to those who need it most might be the perfect way to balance your time at home.

Exercising

Of course it's nice to stay in shape for vanity reasons, but exercise also does wonders for your self-esteem and overall mood. The endorphins released through any sort of exercise oxygenate your brain and reinvigorate your soul. (More on this in Chapter 11.)

Finding a hobby

Identifying what makes your soul come alive, outside of motherhood, is key in maintaining a good balance as a stay-at-home mom. Whether this means crafting, taking up a new sport, reading, cooking, or something else, finding and fostering a hobby that doesn't involve domestic responsibilities creates a space in your life where you can put yourself first for a change. (More on this in Chapter 12.)

Expressing yourself creatively

Although I'm partial to expressing creativity through writing, there are numerous ways to keep your creative juices thriving through motherhood. Consider taking up painting; crafting; singing; playing a musical instrument; writing poetry, fiction, or non-fiction; sculpting; and so on. Creating something out of nothing is a rewarding outlet for the mind and soul.

Starting a business

If the thought of becoming a mompreneur interests you in any capacity, consider your interests and passions and brainstorm different business ideas that might stem from those interests. Although this form of "balance" is not for every stay-at-home mom, many will find an outlet and a business by becoming a mompreneur. And yes, you can still be a good stay-at-home mom and business owner. (More on this in Chapter 13.)

Finding balance

Now that we've recognized our *need* for balance, how do we find it? It's one thing to talk about and try for balance in your new role, but as mothers, we know how difficult it can be to actually obtain it. Days can easily spin into a bit of chaos, and as soon as you check one thing off of your to-do list, something else pops up. You're constantly teetering between providing attention and care to your babe(s), keeping the household functioning, and finding time for yourself. Achieve the mythical balance that all moms seek through: scheduling, prioritizing, enlisting outside help, saying no, defending your "me time," and embracing life's ebb and flow.

Create a schedule

Every Sunday, I take 10 minutes of my evening to craft a schedule for the week ahead. Creating a schedule may seem like a silly thing to do as a stay-at-home because you may think you don't have anything worthy of scheduling—no big meetings, events, or deadlines to dictate your days. However, by creating weekly schedules, you give yourself the power to carve out time for yourself and to be mindful of how you spend your time every day. If I don't plan fun outings with my kiddos, "me time," date nights, or dinners with friends, they will never happen, balance will never fully be achieved, and I will become a slave to my domestic responsibilities. There is power and clarity in creating weekly schedules that foster a balanced lifestyle.

Prioritize

Each Sunday as I'm finalizing my calendar for the upcoming week, I also list my priorities for that week. This may seem simple and obvious, but by listing everything you want to accomplish each week on a piece of paper or typing it on the notes app on your phone, and numbering your items in order of importance—1 being very important and 10 being the least important—you'll be able to clearly see what you need to devote your attention to each week.

Enlist outside help

Read this carefully: Being a stay-at-home mom does not mean that you've become Superwoman and can now accomplish everything that needs to get done on your own. Sure, you don't go into a job every day, but don't forget you *are* working hard every day. Identify the weak points in your life and daily routine where you feel the most stretched or stressed about and brainstorm ways to enlist help in those areas. Just like in business, if a project is too big for one person to tackle alone, a committee or a team is formed to work on it together. Stay-at-home moms need support, too. After all, isn't raising tiny humans the biggest "project" you've ever been given?

Scenarios

- You're feeling overwhelmed with "two under two" and are struggling to find time to cook dinner at night.

Look into meal delivery services a couple times per week to lessen your stress load.

- After deciding to start a small side business from home, you don't have time to deep clean the house regularly. Look into hiring a cleaning person or crew to come and take over the deep cleaning responsibilities once a month or every other week.

- Can't find the space for "me time" to recharge your batteries that are running on low? Enlist your family, friends, or a trusted sitter to watch the kids for a couple hours while you focus on filling your cup back up.

Resist the urge to feel guilty about enlisting help in any area that you are struggling with. You only have two hands and 24 hours in a day. Asking for help is not surrendering or failing in your role; it's making a smart decision to strengthen your life and the well-being of your family in the areas that are faltering.

Practice saying "no"

Apparently there's this wide-spread rumor that stay-at-home moms have a lot of free time on our hands. Sometimes friends who are working moms, our partners, or other friends and family may start asking for favors because they think we now have the time to help them, especially during the workweek when we're "not working." As a natural-born people-pleaser it's always been hard for me to say no and feel like I've let someone down. But I've realized, especially during my time as a stay-at-home mom, my time is precious and my plate is full. I've embraced saying no, and *let me tell you,* it's liberating.

Defend your "me time"

When daily lives become too busy and something needs to give, "me time" is always the first to go. You probably felt guilty about even scheduling any "me time" in the first place, so when the time came to lighten up your load, you almost felt relieved to remove the "me time" from your to-do list.

But perhaps you're looking at "me time" all wrong. It seems, on the surface, to be a selfish act. *I want to go and get a manicure and pedicure because my nails are in rough shape and it relaxes me.* At first glance, this is a selfish statement because you're using words such as, "I want," "my," and "me." Words that might make you feel uncomfortable after leading a life dedicated to caring for others. But this is where you'll need to look at your "me time" from a different perspective and uncover its true purpose.

Carving out time for yourself to do something you enjoy is also bettering yourself for your children and your family. A refreshed, focused, happy mommy is 1,000 percent better than a run-down, depleted, has-nothing-left-to-give mommy.

Defend the things that fill your cup back up so you can turn around and pour 100 percent of yourself into your family.

Embrace life's ebb and flow

Allow some things to slip while other things fall into place. Some seasons of life require you to tip the scale in one direction or the other. One week, you may need more "me time" because your husband was traveling for work the week prior and just one hour at the gym is not going to fill your cup back up enough in order to turn around and pour it into your children and your household again. You may need to carve out additional time for yourself. Conversely, you may need to devote 100 percent of your attention to your child who is sick with the flu one week, so the gym or your volunteer work may not be in the cards during that time.

Circumstances arise and life happens while we're busy making schedules and checklists. Stay in tune with your soul and listen to what it needs as you navigate motherhood, always striving for balance but also realizing the ebb and flow of life.

Exercise: Organize and prioritize

Create a calendar for you and your family for the next week and make sure to schedule "me time" at least once (maybe more, depending on your unique ebb and flow).

Make a to-do list for your upcoming week and prioritize your activities so you can stay on track and feel accomplished at the end of each week.

Identify areas of your life in which you feel stretched too thin and write them down. Next to each, write a possible solution and look into how you can enlist help in that area of your life.

Affirmations

- My journey as a stay-at-home mom is unique.
- I'm not defined by the stereotypes that come with staying home.
- I have the power to carve out "me time" in our weekly routine.
- I fill my cup back up for me and for my family.
- I am a supermom but I know I can't do it all alone.
- Asking for help strengthens my family.
- Finding balance allows me to thrive.
- I am just the kind of mom my family needs.

Chapter 7

Find Your Mom Tribe

*"Behind every successful woman is a tribe of other
successful women who have her back."*
—Unknown

S ipping champagne and relishing the time we dedicated to
our sacred moms-only brunch, we went around the table
and each shared our goals for the new year.

"If I'm being honest," one of my closest mom friends
started, "I'm working on building up my confidence again.
I've somehow lost all confidence since becoming 'just a
mom.'" This coming from a woman who exuded confidence
and power in her past career life. The weight of her words
hung thick in the air while the rest of us processed the details
of the confession and realized it reflected in ourselves.

"I feel the same way," another friend whispered, choking
on welling tears.

"Same," I admitted. We all sat in silence for a few moments before the power of the mama tribe kicked into high gear.

"But we're all amazing moms and extraordinary human beings!" one of us exclaimed.

"It's true—we pour 110 percent of ourselves into our kids, our spouses, our friends. We should be confident in the holy work we're doing, raising a family," another reminded us.

This is what we did. When one of us was having a hard day, a weak moment, or needed a pat on the back—we showed up, we listened without judgment, we offered our best advice, and reminded each other of our strengths and general awesomeness.

The women at that table each came into my life at different times—some old friends who happened to have babies around the same time as me, others I met in a mommy and me group, and others I picked up at random places like a toddler gymnastics class, the park, or through other mom friends. I saw these women at least once a week—at play dates, events, or birthday parties; we were raising our children together, but most importantly, we had each other's backs along the way.

• • • • • • • •

"Well, we should get the babes and our dogs together— we live so close." I felt my voice shaking with nerves as I decided to just go for it. "Do you want to come over for a play date next Tuesday morning?" There it was. My very first mom pick-up. I wondered if I came across too desperate or maybe I had misjudged our friendly encounter at the meet-up group and the potential for a real friendship.

"Sure! We'd love to!" my new mom friend said with an enthusiasm that made me sigh with relief.

The following Tuesday, I woke up early and cleaned my house, made sure the coffee was hot and ready, and even baked muffins to offer up to my new friend. I strategically scattered toys on the living room carpet, even though our babies were only a few months old and mostly just laid under play mats. I bought doggy bones for each of our dogs to keep them busy while we chatted and cooed over our new babies.

I didn't know much about this new friend other than she also had a 3-month-old baby girl and a dog, recently re-signed from her teaching career to become a stay-at-home mom, and she lived just a few blocks away. That was enough common ground for me to pull the trigger on a play date, just the two of us. I envisioned a wonderful friendship stem-ming from our commonalities and, perhaps, a new ally in this mothering gig.

As soon as the doorbell rang and I opened the door, the chaos began. It turns out 3-month-old babies are nothing com-pared to two dogs meeting for the first time. My golden retriever and her Chihuahua got off to a rough start, chasing each other through the house while barking loudly. When I pulled the bones out to distract them from each other, they fought over them in a not-so-playful way, resulting in my dog being put on a time-out in the backyard. While our visit was nice, it was also hectic as my 80-pound golden retriever continued to throw himself at our sliding glass doors, barking, trying to come inside. Then one baby began crying, followed by the other, and before I knew it, there was so much barking and crying going on that a conversation was impossible, I forgot to offer up coffee or a muffin, and our time together was cut too short.

Welp, that did not go as planned, I thought. But through the chaos and realness of that first play date, we were able to cut through the surface of perfectly cleaned houses and fresh baked muffins, and see each other as we really were—both smack-dab in the middle of finding our footing as new moms.

We laughed off our first play date and scheduled a new play date, sans dogs. And over time, regular play dates, advice over text, and eventually, our entire families meeting and hitting it off, my vision of fostering a strong friendship with this woman came to fruition.

We still laugh about our first play date together—the awkwardness of it escalated by the chaos. But true friends laugh with you through the mess; they make you feel like your life is not so crazy, because theirs is crazy, too.

· · · · · · · ·

My feet swelled and my stomach growled as I held my 1-year-old's hand and stood in line for a breakfast burrito and a decaf vanilla latte at our local coffee shop. Seven months pregnant with my son, starving, and sweating in the mid-summer heat didn't make for an ideal morning. After placing my order, I lead my daughter over to a little bench under a sliver of shade—some relief from the heat and my large body straining heavily on my ankles. Something didn't feel right. Looking at my daughter, my vision began swirling. *I need water*, I thought. Jumping up from the bench too quickly, I became light-headed and stumbled over my swollen feet before catching myself with my knee and a hand on a nearby table. I sat down again. "Come here, honey, stay close to Mama." I called my husband in panic and told him what was happening. He said he'd leave work right away, but that still meant a 30-minute drive for him to get to us. My next call was to my best mom friend who lived just up the street.

"You're where? Okay, stay right there. I'll be there in five." I think she actually made it in three. Dropped everything to show up, hold my hand, and call my doctor to report my symptoms, comforting my daughter and me, and talking me through it all. She stayed with us until my husband arrived, then offered to watch our daughter while we headed to the hospital.

Thankfully, my baby was fine—I was just a bit dehydrated and overheated with low blood sugar. But I often think about what would have happened if my girlfriend didn't show up in three minutes flat.

This is the power of your mom tribe. Women who show up and fill in the gaps when you need them most. With no parents or parent-in-laws in town, I found my "village" in other moms. Women looking after one another through pregnancy, birth, and raising tiny humans—these women are my people, these people are my lifeline.

Finding new mom friends

Although it's so important to come together during this season of life, it can also be hard or intimidating to find new moms and foster meaningful friendships. Many moms, me included, have compared it to dating again because it requires putting yourself out there and becoming vulnerable to the possibility of rejection. Although the process seems daunting, the rewards are immeasurable. I've made many connections through motherhood, some meaningful friendships that I know will stand the test of time, and others more surface-level, but I've never regretted one relationship. I've never lamented putting myself out there time and time again. I've learned so much from amazing mothers, received support when I needed it the most, and felt less alone on my journey through motherhood.

Toolkit: Where to find new mom friends

Here are some suggestions and resources on where to find your people: mom groups.

- Visit Meetup.com and enter your city and "mommy and me group" to see if there are any groups nearby.
- Join a MOPS (mother's of preschoolers) group in your area.
- Join a mommy group through your community center or church.
    - *"I found a few friends from the parent/child classes at our local city community center program. And,*

> *I did make two great friends in my prenatal PGA class."* —Denise Bonaimo Sarram

- Mommy-and-me classes in your area (music, sign language, Gymboree, gymnastics, dance).

  - *"Library story time. If you go early and stay late, it's easy to strike up natural conversations with other moms who go weekly."* —Molly Flinkman

- Exercise classes where you can bring your baby (mommy and me yoga, barre with baby in a baby carrier, or Fit4Mom classes).

  - *"Mommy and baby yoga class and just putting myself out there. If I was invited to do something with other moms, I would always say yes!"* —Michelle Nelson

  - *"I found my best mom friends at my son's preschool. It is an inclusive school for kids with special needs. I suddenly found moms who got it and it was amazing. We traded tips and laughed about the weird and hard things we found ourselves doing to make life easier."* —Jamie Sumner

- YMCAs in your area
  - *"Coffee shops! If they like good coffee then we definitely already have two things in common: kids and coffee."* —Sarah Eschenbach Freeman

- Family-friendly events in your area. Save your community's event calendar.

- ° *"A lot of my friends have had kids around the same time but I have also met a lot of other moms through Instagram who have small businesses, too, and juggle the same types of things I do."* —Julia Wheeler

- The park
  - ° *"Walking the neighborhood with your stroller and seeing another mom with a stroller—saying hi and a friendly compliment can go a long way in making their day and starting a friendship."* —Kate Heyde

- Support groups in your area (new parenting groups, breastfeeding groups, baby sleep classes, mindful parenting classes, and so on).
  - ° *"I started a local workout class in my neighborhood so I could make friends."* —Lisa Druxman

- Apps for moms. Peanut is the new Tinder for mom friends—swipe left or right and connect with your perfect mom match.
  - ° *"Chatting with the other mothers as we waited for our children in dance class."* —Marisa Svalstedt

- Baby aisles at Target or your local grocer. Swapping notes or asking for advice about baby products is the perfect icebreaker.
  - ° *"I started finding mom groups online. Even though I have yet to meet with any of the ladies it's nice to know there are others going through what I'm going through and have them to talk to during the day."* —Adrian Wells

- Create your own group in your area for mommy and me meet-ups and invite local moms to join.

I started Mom Tribe, a group for new moms to get together without the kiddos and enjoy fun events, networking, and camaraderie. I run the San Diego chapter but would love to help you start one in your own city. Visit *thetribemagazine.com/events* for more information.

Tried and true pick-up lines

Although using a pick-up line to start a new conversation with a potential mom friend seems weird, and strangely reminiscent of your dating days, it could also hold the key to unlocking a friendship with another mom. The same nerves that kept you guessing during your dating years come into play while wondering things like, "Does she like me, too?" "Does this have the potential to grow into a real relationship?" "Am I coming on too strong over text?"

Then there's the whole "putting yourself out there" through conversation starters, searching for common ground, and getting each other's phone numbers. As uncomfortable as those first few "mommy pick-ups" can be, you'll likely start becoming more confident with your conversation starters and identifying like-minded mamas who you'll click with.

I asked some moms to share their tried-and-true pick-up lines that worked when recruiting new mom friends:

- *"I love your leggings!"* (Because every mom wears leggings.) —Sarah Eschenbach Freeman
- *"How old is your kiddo? He/she is so cute!"* —Stephanie Byrd
- *"I find that it's often easy to strike up a conversation by mentioning something you notice that is positive about their child, whether it's an outgoing personality, winning smile, fearless nature, or large vocabulary. All children are beautiful, so it's not difficult to let a fellow mom know that you see something noteworthy about their child. I think most moms are happy to talk about how amazing their children are. I know I am."* —Marisa Svalstedt
- *"I usually take a deep breath and go right for it: We'd love to have you over for a play date sometime! Can I have your phone number?"* —Molly Flinkman

Exercise: Pick up a new mom

Throughout the next week, choose an outing or place where you know you'll run into other moms, and practice your pick-up lines on at least two new moms. Bonus points if you get their digits!

Friends every mom needs on her team

I've always found that I was attracted to different types of friends throughout my life because each brought something unique to the table, which made my life feel balanced and diverse. The same holds true for motherhood. Life suddenly becomes very one-dimensional if we only have a bunch of cookie-cutter mom friends who all act the same, give the same advice, and serve the same purpose in our lives. It's much better to befriend moms of different backgrounds, and personality types, each offering different strengths in your friendships. Here are a few types of mom friends that are beneficial to have on your team:

1. **The type A highly organized mom.** If you ever forget something while you're out and about with your little ones, no worries, she has you covered. Her diaper bag is carefully packed and organized by food products (healthy snacks), diaper supplies (all organic), and several back-up clothes (coordinating, of course). Her minivan must be vacuumed at the end of each day because there's not a Cheerio in sight, and she's always put-together with an ironed blouse, trendy jeans, and applied makeup. #momgoals

2. **The go-with-the-flow mom.** She's usually down for a last-minute play date, or not—it's cool! She may be on to something with her laissez-fair attitude toward motherhood and life in general. Because you can't sweat the small stuff while raising tiny humans.

3. **The kids' party mom.** She's always throwing some sort of kids' party whether it's a cookie decorating party just in time for Christmas, an Easter egg hunt,

or a Valentine's Day card exchange. And you love her because she's entertaining your kids and checking things off of your to-do list with her brilliant, and timely, themes.

4. **The girls night mom.** This mom is always advocating for and planning girls nights. And thank goodness for her dedication to the cause, because otherwise months would pass before your next get-together, sans kiddos.

5. **The Pinterest mom.** When not baking amazing, kid-friendly, healthy recipes for her tiny crew, she's busy sewing costumes or crafting party favors. She's a walking Pinterest board and you hope some of her creativeness will rub off on you, or at least inspire you, at the next play date.

6. **The working mom.** No one says stay-at-home moms can only befriend other stay-at-home moms. (Please, let's not add fuel to the mommy wars!) Working moms are great to have in your circle because they have a pulse on the outside world and may bring a breath of fresh air and new discussion topics into your world normally consumed with only baby talk.

7. **The bestie mom.** This is your go-to-gal, the one who knows all your secrets and doesn't judge you for any of them. You don't have to clean your house before she comes over, and you can share your most intimate thoughts with each other. This mom is more like family.

Toolkit: How to start a mom group in your area

Many moms I've talked to expressed disappointment in not finding any mommy meet-up groups in their immediate area, or not clicking with the moms they had met. In these situations, I suggest starting your own mommy meet-up group. Here's how:

1. **Decide on your niche.** You may find that you're not connecting with other moms you've met because your paths through motherhood don't align. Perhaps your kids are different ages or your interests and values just don't mesh. Identifying your own niche for a mom group will allow you to attract moms who are on similar paths through motherhood. Make your group as detailed as "Stay-at-home moms who are having trouble breastfeeding their newborns" or as broad as "Moms with new babies born in 2017." Or perhaps, you only want to meet moms within a five-mile radius of your home. You can control all the parameters around starting your own group.

2. **Find your platform.** Sites like Meetup.com provide a turnkey solution to starting your own mommy group. You can set you parameters, push it live, and wait for moms to find you based on your location and the pre-requisites of your group.

    You may also use a Facebook group where you can invite a couple of your mom friends to join the group and then encourage them to invite their friends, and so on and so on, until you have a big network in your area. Word of mouth works wonders in spreading the news about a cool new moms groups in the area.

If you're not interested in in-person meet-ups but would rather create more of a support group for moms (also open to those beyond your immediate area), Facebook groups are also a great way to connect with similar moms. Create a group for moms with children who have special needs, or moms who are interested in crafting, cooking, or starting their own businesses from home. You can truly dream up any type of mom group you'd like, and connect with like-minded mamas.

3. **Network and marketing.** The success of your mom group will depend on reaching the right types of moms. Think about where you like to hang out, online or offline, and do some networking and marketing in those areas. Post a flyer in your local coffee shop or at your local library, create a meet-up, and upload it to your city's events page. You can even create a small $5 Facebook ad and target a very specific mom demographic online, inviting them to join your group.

4. **Turn it into a business.** If you're more business-minded, you can even turn your mom group into a small event business. Seek out fun venues, plan more

elaborate events, and obtain event sponsors who are looking to reach the local mom market. You can make money by charging a small fee for each event, or obtaining event sponsorships. This is a win-win because you'll be offering fun events for moms to attend, and paying yourself for your time spent planning the events.

Exercise: Find your tribe

Sign-up for a mommy-meet up group in your area, mommy and me class, or look into starting one of your own.

Fostering meaningful relationships in motherhood

Once you start getting the hang of making new friends through the common ground of motherhood, it's important to also form more meaningful relationships. Deeper relationships happen when we strip back the façade of our Instagram-worthy lives and allow others to see our true selves—the good, the bad, the ugly, and the really ugly. Motherhood naturally lends itself to these meaningful relationships because there's nothing more personal than connecting with someone else while both raising tiny humans. There's an unspoken and immediate bond between mothers because we're all working hard at raising the next generation, together.

At your next get-together, instead of immediately jumping into conversations about your children and their eating and sleeping habits or developmental milestones, try looking at each other and asking, "How are you, really?" Most moms won't offer up the very core of their worries and hardships they're experiencing in their roles, unless you ask them in a heartfelt way that shows that you truly care.

Try offering more in-depth pieces of yourself, too, in order to make others feel comfortable about sharing more intimate details from their own lives. You'll need these deep-rooted friendships for support and camaraderie through your stay-at-home motherhood journey and the real life that lives behind the Instagram filters.

Exercise: Take your relationships to the next level

Take one of your surface mom friendships to the next level by offering up something personal about yourself, and letting your friend know that you're a safe, nonjudgmental zone where she can share personal information with you, too. Don't forget to ask the harder questions, like, "How are you, really?"

Affirmations

- There is power in a good mom tribe.
- It takes a village to raise tiny humans.

- I'm at my best when I feel supported and when I help support others.
- I attract what I put out into the world.
- I am open to attracting and fostering new friendships.
- I have a lot to offer a friendship.
- I am an amazing friend.

Chapter 8

Life Without Raises and Praise: Redefining Success

"Strive not to be a success. But rather to be of value."
—Albert Einstein

Possibly one of the biggest hurdles from career to staying home is accepting life without external rewards, as you're accustomed to receiving them. In your past career life, your dedicated efforts were rewarded every two weeks with a paycheck, maybe every quarter or half-year mark with a performance review, and perhaps every year or couple years with an increase in pay, bonus, or promotion. Add to this shower of external rewards: regular complements from your boss or peers and the immediate gratification of checking big projects off your list. All of these external rewards stack up and feed your ego in a career, making you feel important and valued in the hard work you're completing every day.

So, where are the external rewards for stay-at-home moms? How do you find encouragement within your new role?

....

"I had to learn that even though I am not contributing financially, I still hold value within the family, and I do not need to sacrifice who I am as a person because I made the decision to stay home." —Beth Robinson

....

With no paychecks, performance reviews, bonuses, promotions, or regular pats on the back, how do you feel important and valued in the hard work you're doing day in and day out as a stay-at-home mom?

During my five-year stint at my dream job as a marketing manager with Hyatt Hotels:

- I received two promotions and four raises.
- I received regular recognition and some awards for producing quality work.
- I took pride in keeping my projects in motion and seeing them through to completion.
- I was confident that the work I produced was valued, and that in turn made me feel important in life.

During my three-year stint at my new dream job, as a stay-at-home mom:

- I have yet to be promoted and raises don't exist when you're not getting paid.
- I've received zero awards and very little recognition.

- I'm not always confident in the work I produce; I question every motherly decision and then question it again and overanalyze it because this is not some work project, these are the lives of two adorable little humans, and I'm responsible for keeping them alive and thriving.

- I hardly feel valued and that, in turn, sometimes makes me feel unimportant in life.

About six months into my new life as a stay-at-home mom, I learned this: The rewards often take time to realize and the encouragement comes from within.[1]

....

"[I had to realize] that being home was a job. Sometimes I felt I wasn't contributing. I was so used to working, bringing in money, that to stay home and go to the park while my husband was working seemed frivolous. I needed to get over that." —Lisa Druxman

....

Flip your lens inward. You have the power to give yourself the encouragement and motivation you need in order to succeed in this role. Let that sink in for a moment.

This was hard for me at first, having been conditioned to receiving monetary external rewards as a direct result of my hard work throughout my career. It took some time to train my brain to replace that need for external reinforcement with internal strength and confidence, a *new* currency, if you will.

"Work was validation in so many ways.... But when I became a mom, not one of my three kids under three was patting me on the back and leaving Starbucks gift cards on my desk. My validation was that we all survived another day. I had to learn to stop seeking my worth from outside sources. I had to realize that I could 'validate' my own existence. I am a warrior mom and wife and writer. I know this without anyone else needing to tell me. It's still nice when they do, though." —Jamie Sumner

A new currency that resonates

The Pew Research Center conducted a recent study on how mothers rate their own parenting. From this study, they concluded that stay-at-home moms rated their parenting significantly lower than working mothers, despite the fact that they were spending more of their time on childcare.[2]

Could this be because stay-at-home moms don't fully recognize the importance of their roles and the difference they're making in their child's/children's lives? Could it be because stay-at-home moms don't know how to classify their daily tasks as accomplishments?

"For a while I didn't feel a sense of self-worth because I wasn't allowing myself to change my idea of what providing for my family meant. It took well over a year to finally realize the necessity, and importance of what

I accomplish every day for my child, as well as my husband, and that despite not receiving a paycheck from some corporate entity, I am working very hard in the most important role I've ever had." —Marisa Svalstedt

Your new paycheck

It's hard to notice how much you're actually accomplishing when you're in the daily grind of raising tiny humans. Begin by really studying the work you do as a stay-at-home mom. Let's start with the bread and butter—the work you do every day that simply meets the basic needs of your babies/children: feeding, changing diapers, bathing, and making sure they get enough sleep every day. Although these things seem simple, understand that your tiny human(s) depend on you, quite entirely, to meet these basic needs for survival. Give yourself credit for this important work. You are helping your kiddo(s) live and thrive day-by-day, hour-by-hour, minute-by-minute. Your very presence and dedication is meeting their need for survival. Bank this as your base paycheck as a stay-at-home mom. This stuff counts in a big way.

Your new bonus

Now, let's discuss the exceptional things you do every single day—the things that you may not even count as exceptional because you do them without thinking twice. That's the magic of motherhood—putting 110 percent of yourself into raising your children, and not even realizing the extraordinary work you're actually accomplishing.

Things like comforting and rocking your crying baby throughout the night, bandaging and kissing your toddler's boo-boos, carefully planning and cooking nutritious meals for your kiddos to ensure each food group is included in daily diets, managing health and wellness by scheduling doctor appointments, getting second opinions on diagnostics, and tirelessly researching on your own to ensure you make the right health decisions on behalf of your children. And don't forget how you also shape young minds by leading by example, teach manners and kindness in everyday situations, foster learning through developmental activities and experiences, and constantly instill your family values in your next of kin, helping them stay on track and thriving through each new stage.

This type of exceptional mothering often has no immediate gratification where you'll notice your thorough nurturing and guidance immediately reflected in your children. The delayed reactions make it hard to trace and bank as a job well done.

And chances are, this vigilant nurturing and calculated guidance is not glorified for all to bare witness, and mostly happens behind closed doors for only you and your children to see. So, *see* it. Acknowledge your hard work and unwavering constancy. Count this as the best bonus you've ever received. Your dedicated presence and parenting is making a big difference in your child's life and future, and the special relationship you're establishing along the way is a true gift.

"*When I was working as a nurse, I could feel confident that I was making a difference to the people I cared for.... While I know that raising children is also good and important, sometimes it feels less that way. I don't get to see end results...I spend a lot of time shoving toys into bins and wiping up spilled milk, only to have it be undone moments later. When I focus on the tasks of staying at home, I often feel unfulfilled. I have to focus on the relationship I have with my sons to feel content.*" —Lorren Lemmons

Rewards

You most likely won't see the immediate effects of your hard work raising tiny humans. But when they do surface, and they will, the satisfaction in seeing your committed parenting and guidance reflected in your child/children is the reward of a lifetime. It's worth the wait and a million times better than any plaque or acknowledgement received in your past career life. The following are a few examples:

- When you notice how your baby stops crying as soon as you pick him up, you've created a safe space for him with your simple touch.

- When your daughter takes her first steps or starts stringing together her first words into sentences, you helped encourage that.

- When you see your toddler kiss her "babies" on the forehead and rock them to sleep ever so gently, you showed her that love.

- When your son begins recognizing shapes and recites the alphabet proudly, you helped teach him that.
- When your toddler uses "please" and "thank you" without any prompt, you instilled those manners through your careful guidance.
- When your daughter shows the confidence to go up to a little boy at the park and begin playing with him on her own, you fostered that confidence and those relationship-building skills.

Allow these rewards to feed your soul and replace any need for an external reward through a paycheck. This is your hard work paying off. You're doing amazing things, mama.

....

"The hardest thing for me was learning to disconnect my self-worth from my to-do list. Most days, my big accomplishments aren't things I can quantify or cross off. I successfully handle tantrums or keep my cool during a meltdown. I love and I cuddle and I try to be there for my children. It's hard to see immediate results from this kind of thing but they have value anyway."
—Jess Hernandez

....

Encouragement

Collect all of the rewards you're now banking as a stay-at-home mom and allow them to fill your soul and fuel your own encouragement along your journey. By channeling these rewards into a currency that resonates, you'll have the power to propel your own encouragement from within. You'll stop needing or searching for external encouragement to keep going or to feel "accomplished." Pat yourself on the back and give yourself credit for achievements big and small—it all matters. Combined, it's painting a beautiful picture of your family's unique journey and your children's adolescence and memories in the making.

Performance review

I always liked performance reviews in my past corporate life because it gave me a chance to not only hear from my superior on how he or she felt I was performing, but also provided me the opportunity to take pause and reflect on my own performance—giving myself props for big projects I accomplished and identifying where I needed to step up my game or deliver extra attention.

I've found performance reviews to also be helpful in parenting. Although you don't have a boss to report to (although, most toddlers *can* be considered tiny bosses at times), schedule a meeting with yourself. Allow the space and time to take a pause from your daily duties as a stay-at-home mom and evaluate your own performance. This will give you the opportunity to step back and recognize your accomplishments (helping fuel your own encouragement), identify areas where you need to focus or redirect attention, and mindfully set new goals for the next quarter.

Recently, when I took pause for my own performance review, I realized I needed to give more undivided attention to my daughter as she was having a tough time transitioning with her new baby brother in the family mix. Within my daily activities and responsibilities as a stay-at-home mom, I had failed to catch the reasoning behind her new bad behavior and sour moods. When I allowed myself the space to step back and asses my mothering, it was clear that she needed more one-on-one time with me—time I wasn't currently providing. So, I set goals to provide just that. I scheduled mommy/daughter dates for some upcoming weekends when my husband was home to watch my son. We got our nails done together, we went out to lunch, and just talked over pizza. Talk is a loose word, as I was mostly fielding millions of questions from her inquisitive little mind. And over time her daily behavior improved, directly resulting from me fulfilling a real need that she had but couldn't yet verbalize. Without my performance review for myself, I may have overlooked this important need of hers.

....

Counseling advice

"The two main things that stand out for me in this chapter are its 'strength-based' approach and its modeling and encouragement of self-compassion. This shift from working outside the home to working inside the home is a big one. In one arena, you have a clear job description and cues and feedback along the way to help guide you in your growth. In the other arena, the job-description is massively broad and the cues and feedback tend to be more abstract and unclear ('Why is my baby crying?' 'What is creating this new behavior?'

'Let's try peas and see if that is yummy.') Stopping to reflect and notice—I mean really notice—your hard work, nurtures the growth of knowing your intrinsic worth. Does it feel good to hear from your mate/family/ friends that they see the hard work you do and are proud of you? Yes! Of course! It is the icing on the cake and the cake is what you are giving yourself. Self-compassion is a constant in this work as sometimes recognizing an area that needs improvement may tempt the old stories of shame ('Shouldn't I have known this already?' 'Why aren't I better at [fill in the blank]?' 'I suck at this'). With loving-kindness, acknowledge these areas of growth and nurture this growth with patience, creativity, and care—just as you would for your child." —Karen Simms, mental health counselor

Exercise: Meeting with the boss

Plan regular (quarterly or bi yearly) performance reviews for yourself where you carve out the time and space to consider the following:

1. **What have I accomplished since my last review?** List everything big and small (the "paycheck," meeting simple needs type of stuff; and the "bonus," exceptional mothering stuff).

2. **What areas of my parenting can I identify that may need more attention?** List ways you can help

strengthen or improve these areas of your parenting. Create an action plan to refocus your attention.

3. **What do I want to be mindful of while parenting over the next few months?** Set goals for the next quarter or half-year, include any action plans you may have created from the question above, and list new goals that you'd like to work toward over the next several months.

Affirmations

- My encouragement comes from my strength and drive from within.
- I know my own worth and am proud of my accomplishments.
- I am dedicated to parenting my tiny humans with intention every day.
- Big and small accomplishments can be found in my everyday parenting. It all matters.
- My job as a stay-at-home mom is important. My work matters.
- I give myself credit for a job well done. I'm making a big difference in my child's/children's lives.
- I am constantly bettering myself for my family.
- I give my child/children exactly what they need as they grow and thrive.

Chapter 9

Addressing Stigma and Society's View of Stay-at-Home Moms

"In a culture that relentlessly promotes avarice and excess as the good life, a person happy doing his own work is usually considered an eccentric, if not a subversive. Ambition is only understood if it's to rise to the top of some imaginary ladder of success.... To invent your own life's meaning is not easy, but it's still allowed, and I think you'll be happier for the trouble."
—Bill Watterson

"So, I hear you've officially retired!" My neighbor's smug grin and uneducated words struck a wrong chord with me. Clearly, he classified being a stay-at-home mom with retirement and leisure—perhaps some casual rounds of golf, tennis lessons, or lying by the pool reading a novel and sipping a mai tai. Ha! The contrast between retirement and my reality—taking care of a colicky newborn—added fuel to my internal rage.

I was about three months into my new role, drowning in it, quite honestly, and not yet confident enough to put him in his place. So, I laughed it off and replied as gracefully as

I could: "Yes, I've retired from my career for now, and I'm home with my daughter. Yes, it's going well. Yes, she's doing great." At least I had my shtick down.

His words haunted me and continued to irk me for longer than I care to admit, because I knew his statement symbolized a large part of society's views of stay-at-home moms and it reflected, in turn, all the ambiguity I harbored about myself and my choice. My good friend self-doubt showed up and did what she does best—flooded my mind with self-deprecating questions: *Did others think I was lazy? Did they realize how much I had sacrificed and how hard I was actually working? Was I wasting my education? Had I blown my chance to succeed in corporate America should I return back to the workforce?*

Raising a tiny human was the hardest work I had ever done, but how do you convey that to my neighbor who doesn't have kids of his own? How do I convey that to others who have already made up their minds about stay-at-home moms, our choice, and "lifestyle"?

....

"I worked long hours as a teacher but I could go home. Being a SAHM is a 24/7 job." —Stephanie Byrd

....

I'd like to take this opportunity to climb up on my soapbox for a moment, megaphone in hand—*tap, tap, is this thing on?* I have something to say about society's thoughts on stay-at-home moms, our importance, and how we've evolved since the stereotypes that began back in the 1950s (read: almost 70 years ago). Ready? This is going to be revolutionary: *I don't care.*

I don't care what you think of me, or my decision, or what you think I do every day. I don't care because I know my truth. I know the realities and details of life as a stay-at-home mom—the all-consuming, beautiful, messy, selfless work I do every single day, and through the night, and sometimes into the wee-hours of the morning. Yes, I know it very well.

In the beginning, I did care what others thought. I *really* cared. I recited my past resume to anyone who would listen to prove that I was an educated and motivated person. But I've developed some thick skin since that encounter with my neighbor, because, sadly, comments like his are a dime a dozen. I also realized something important along the way: The only person I need to be able to face every day is myself, and I'm the only one who will ever understand how hard I work in this role. I owe my soul the peace that comes with embracing my decision to stay home with my children, raising them with intention 24 hours a day, 7 days a week, and knowing deep down that my work at home matters.

Battling outside opinions

It's hard to say for sure if my marginalized feelings about my role as a stay-at-home mom stemmed from within or from outside opinions. Perhaps it was a mixture of both. After choosing to stay home with my baby, I was blindsided

by the unsolicited comments and awkward encounters I began experiencing. My neighbor's remarks about my new "life
of retirement" were only the first drops in an oncoming tidal
wave of other comments that always left me feeling less-than:
"What do you do all day?" "Don't you get bored?" "Are you
worried about finding a job later down the road?" "I could
never leave my job." And then there were the ones that made
me feel guilty or undeservingly privileged: "Must be nice."
"Wow, how lucky are you?" "I wish we could afford to do
that."

Perhaps, deep down, I did feel guilty for staying home.
All of the questions and comments pointed at me were also
questions that I was battling internally. These outside opinions only amplified my deteriorating confidence surrounding
my decision to stay home. However, I realized that the only
reason these comments were making me feel less-than was
because I was letting them. In order to stand up to outside
judgment and brush it off, I first needed to come to peace
with my new role, within my *own* soul.

....

*"I was very proud of my job—I worked hard and
felt that I was doing good in the world as a pediatric
nurse. With this career, when I met people who would
ask where I worked, I felt like my answer always led
to interesting conversations. However, when we moved
from the city where my husband attended graduate
school and started over in a new city (when I became a
stay-at-home mom), as I met people who asked what I*

*did, I realized that I didn't have this immediate conver-
sation starter of my work anymore. I would meet these
highly intelligent, capable women who were my husband's coworkers, and while I saw myself standing on
similar ground with them as a woman with an important and difficult job, I realized they perceived me very
differently."* —Lorren Lemmons

The "mommy wars"

Prior to becoming a mom, I wasn't privy to the "mommy
wars" and the never-ending jabs between working moms and
stay-at-home moms. I remember when I was a brand new
mom; I belonged to a mommy group full of other brand new
moms (working moms and stay-at-home moms). One day,
a stay-at-home mom posted a park meet-up date at 10 a.m.
on a Wednesday. One of the working moms in our group
commented on the event: "Some of us have to work at that
time." I felt the awkwardness through my computer screen,
and every mom on either side of that loaded comment felt
the weight of those words.

Honestly, I can see it from both sides: Working moms
probably felt guilty that their day jobs were getting in the way
of experiencing fun, new meet-ups with their baby and other
mommy-baby duos. When the working moms in the group
saw that event meet-up at the park, it probably felt like an ex-
clusion or a reminder of harbored guilt about their new roles
as working moms. On the other side of the coin, the stay-at-
home mom who posted that event was likely just looking for

some adult interaction to break up her week, which was now filled with very little. That event, to her, was a lifeline in her new role. And all the stay-at-home moms who then read the working mom's comment, "*Some of us* have to work" couldn't help but feel those words directed at them—making them feel in some way, privileged or guilty that they *could* meet up at that time.

All being new moms in that group, fresh off of our decisions to either stay home with the kids or return to our careers, each battling the pros and cons and true weight of those decisions—the words "some of us" drew the line in the sand right then and there. It was our first taste of the mommy wars. The first taste of events and word choices that could be interpreted in any way that the receiver was already battling internally—our self-deprecating thoughts reflected in the words or actions of another.

I know many of us walked away from that online encounter with a newfound sense of a very real divide between working moms and stay-at-home moms. One that many of us hadn't considered before. I know I hadn't.

See each other

I won't sit here and pretend to know what it's like to be a working mom, but I do want to say this to the working mamas: *I see you.* I see you kissing your children goodbye every day, and having to miss out on some of the big stuff and good stuff of raising tiny humans. I see how there can be complex feelings and big sacrifices laced within your decision to return to your career. I see you and see how hard you're working day in and day out—juggling all of the emotions, all of the tasks, all of the responsibilities with raising a family. *I see you.*

Stay-at-home moms: I see you and I feel you, because I *am* you. I see you putting your career on hold and staying home with your children every day. I see you there through the mundane and trying times of raising tiny humans. I know the complex feelings and big sacrifices laced within your decision to stay home. I see you and see how hard you're working day in and day out—juggling all of the emotions, all of the tasks, all of the responsibilities with raising a family. *I see you.*

What if

What if we started battling against this notion of "mommy wars" by first winning the struggles we're each fighting within? What if we came to peace with our own decisions before muttering hurtful or loaded remarks to other moms? What if we realized that there's not just a one-size-fits-all journey through motherhood—that this role fits us each differently? What if we acknowledged that every mom, regardless if they work outside the home or inside the home, is doing the best she can for her family? What if we realized there are pros and cons to staying home and returning to a career? What if we joined together in unity instead of tearing each other down in hostility? What if we supported each other in each of our chosen paths? What if we celebrated each other? What if the mother in me acknowledges the mother in you and we lifted each other up?

Exercise: Make another mom's day

Choose at least two friends—include a working mom and a stay-at-home mom—and let them know that you see them. Either face-to-face at the next play date, over a heartfelt text message, or an old-school handwritten letter, let them know you see how hard they're working raising their families and keeping all the balls in the air. Let each one know that she's doing a good job and she is a *good mom*.

Battling stigma

It's sad that the only stay-at-home moms portrayed in the media are bickering housewives with bottomless bank accounts, or commercials associated with mops and cleaning products. It's no wonder there is no value placed in our roles. Meanwhile, working moms are portrayed with a cape and called "super mom" for bringing home the bacon and then frying it in the pan. (Note: Working moms definitely deserve that cape, but stay-at-home moms do, too.)

I truly believe that the only way society will stop marginalizing the work of stay-at-home moms is if we, stay-at-home moms, stop letting them. We have the power to define our roles appropriately, and show others how this role should be viewed, respected, and celebrated. But in order to spread this newfound appreciation for stay-at-home moms and sing our worth, we must first do that from within.

Exercise: Shred and redefine

Gather all the stigma and condescending comments or questions you've heard directed at you, portrayed in the media, and any negative thoughts you're battling internally associated with your job as a stay-at-home mom, and write them all down on a piece of paper.

Then, write comebacks to each of these negative comments or questions, in your defense. Feel free to get real angry with it—use profanity, go on a rant, whatever feels good!

Now, take that piece of paper and shred it into tiny pieces. These words don't define you and your role as a stay-at-home mom so you don't need them in your life weighing you down. Trash them.

Finally, take out a new piece of paper and write your own truth. Define yourself, here and now, with the cape you deserve. (Example: I am a hardworking, loving mother who gives my all to raising my children with intention every day.)

Memorize your new truth and don't allow anyone else the power to define you again. Find peace in knowing that you get to write your own truth. Everything else is just background noise.

Knowing your own worth

I've heard it time and time again in response to the question, "What do you do for a living?" (I've been a culprit of saying it, too): "Oh, I'm just a stay-at-home mom." *Just.* Such a small word that labels your life and your work as unimportant. Let's remove "just" from our description, shall we? Mamas, we are so much more than "just."

....

"[It's difficult] feeling like I am 'just a mom' when in fact I have the hardest job in the world. My children are happy and thriving, so I am doing things right!" —Michelle Nelson

....

I've read some articles online that suggest new, updated titles for stay-at-home moms such as "Household Manager" or "Chief Executive Mom" or "Chief Child Wrangler," and so on. Although these are creative and cute, I don't feel the power behind them. I don't take them seriously. And being a stay-at-home mom is a serious role—an important one.

So, let's come up with some strong answers to the question, "What do you do?" I agree that the "staying home" part of the title is outdated and immediately conjures up preconceived images of Miss Suzy Homemaker from the 50s or, maybe even worse, a modern-day desperate housewife. As a society we place great value in doing, creating, and accomplishing. But the words *staying home* don't portray us as doing, creating, accomplishing members of society. So, let's leave "stay at home" out of it. It's null and void in our true roles. Instead, let's try these on for size:

- "I'm a mom." *Period.* There's power in that period. No explanation necessary and no room for slighted words like "just."

- "I'm raising our next generation." Boom. Or, if you want to take it a step further: "I'm raising the next generation of thought leaders/leaders/change-makers/ good humans."

And if the question is, "Do you work?" The answer should always be:

- "**Yes**, I'm a mom."
- "**Yes**, I'm raising our next generation."
- "**Yes**, I'm raising the next generation of thought leaders/ leaders/change-makers/good humans."

Simple. Powerful. Unexpected. Let's quit apologizing for the biggest role we've ever had. Let's quit marginalizing our job of raising tiny humans, one in which we work tirelessly at every day and night. Let's celebrate our roles as caretakers, mind-shapers, and family leaders. Let's exude so much pride in our roles that it has no choice but to rub off on others. The shift in society that we seek starts within us.

Singing your own praise

The biggest disconnects or misconceptions about what a stay-at-home mom does all day are simply because the majority of people in this world are not stay-at-home moms or have never been one. They have no idea what the role looks like from the inside, just as I will never know the ins and outs of being a doctor or a lawyer or an astronaut. One cannot begin to comprehend someone else's job or role unless that person shares her story, her journey, her hardships, and her wins.

Only stay-at-home moms know the truth behind this role: Being a stay-at-home mom is a valuable existence. It's hard work with huge results (you know, raising tiny humans). And you deserve to feel pride in that role.

While you keep your own self-worth close to your heart and soul, don't be afraid to sing your own praise for the world to hear, too. *And why not?* Don't others boast about promotions or new jobs or closing deals in their 9-to-5 jobs? Stay-at-home moms: Don't forget to sing your own praise, too! While society celebrates doing, creating, and achieving, enlighten others about your hard work and dedication to your role as a stay-at-home mom and how you ARE doing, creating, and achieving, every day! Talk about the hard stuff, the stuff you have to overcome behind the beautiful filters and smiling faces on your Instagram account. Let others know that it's difficult and worth it, and you're proud of where you're dedicating your time: to your children. Your pride and passion toward your role will show others how it should be viewed and treated—with the respect and reverence it deserves.

Counseling advice

"In this chapter, the areas of self-worth, empathy, and social activism are explored. Kristin writes about her discomfort and defensiveness when her neighbor compares her working as a mom to retirement then journeys toward self-worth and the ability to not take personal someone else's story about her. In the book by Don Miguel Ruiz, The Four Agreements,

he writes the second agreement as: 'Don't take anything personally. Nothing others do is because of you.
What others say and do is a projection of their own
reality, their own dream. When you are immune to
the opinions and actions of others, you won't be the
victim of needless suffering.' To get here, we must
understand our own uncertainties and doubts that
opened the way for another person's story about us
to be so activating. What they say feels so personal
because it resonates with our internal voice saying,
'See! I knew it was true!'

With self-compassion, look at this internal wound
and untangle what it means, begin to understand
the self-doubt, and redefine your truth: a person of
worthiness on a path of growth and healing. When
we are not coming from our defenses nor taking
personal someone else's stories, we have more room
for empathy. As Kristin writes, 'I see you.' This is the
ability to look beyond the surface action or words
and see the intention, the heart, and even the wounds
of another. As mothers, recognizing this in each other
creates strong connections and community. Coming from a place of worthiness versus defensiveness
allows for authenticity and a voice that will help
change and shape cultural norms and ideas about
motherhood. Singing your praises from this perspective shows others what a stay-at-home mother looks
like: energy, love, hard work, and growth." —Karen
Simms, mental health counselor

Affirmations

- I get to write my own definition.
- My role as a mother is the most important job I've ever had.
- My role as a stay-at-home mom matters.
- I dictate my own self-worth.
- I support all moms on their unique journey through motherhood.
- I am proud of my job as a stay-at-home mom.
- I am confident in my job as a stay-at-home mom.

Chapter 10

Feminism and Opting Out of Career

"Feminism means having a choice. And feminism doesn't care which choices you make, either. Just that you have them."
—Rachel Kadish

When the boxes containing our new barstools arrived one afternoon, I spilled the contents onto our living room rug and studied the assembly instructions with my little helper. Just my humble opinion, but 50 pieces seems a little excessive for simple stools!

After a half-hour trying to puzzle the pieces together, my daughter said in defeat, "Maybe we need Dada to help us."

I laughed because she was probably right—he is more patient than I am with this sort of thing and she's seen him assemble numerous pieces of furniture and toys; this seemed like a "Dad thing." But because she said that out loud, because she thought it, I became determined to put the stools together. "We can do it, B—let's keep trying!"

Suddenly, our Amazon Prime barstools turned into a metaphor for the strength and willpower of all women, everywhere. We were going to build the best damn barstools the world had ever seen! Overboard, I know—but also an opportunity to show my daughter that we girls can use tools and build something out of nothing, with our bare hands.

So we did.

It may have taken us a better part of an afternoon, but we built those stools and high-fived each other as we sat back and admired our work.

"You did it, Mama!" she exclaimed with too much shock in her tone for my liking.

"*We* did it, B! Because we're girls and we rock!" I shot right back.

She smiled knowingly and said, "We *are* girls!"[1]

Contradictory terms

Somehow the idea of being a feminist and a stay-at-home mom felt contradictory to me at first. I'm not financially independent, I rely quite entirely on my husband to support our family financially; I'm not shattering through glass ceilings, I'm likely cleaning them with Windex in the confinements of my own home; and I'm not competing with men on an ascent up the corporate ladder, I've abandoned my hard-earned spot in corporate America for the time being. While women are encouraged to "lean in" to our careers, I've bowed out. I've opted for the more "traditional" role as a "homemaker" and "stay-at-home mom"—all terms and ideas that somehow just don't taste right with "feminist."

However, I strongly believe in equal opportunities for women and want to yell *"Hoo-rah!"* every time I see or hear about a woman who is out there blazing trails for equal rights, equal pay, and equal social status. I come from a family of strong, independent women—my grandmother was the breadwinner for her family, my mother was a single mom working and raising three girls, and prior to becoming a mom myself, I fought tooth and nail for my seat at the board table. The movement resonates with me deeply. I *am* a feminist.

But now, I'm not on those frontlines—I'm on the home front. So, I posed the questions to myself: *Where do I belong in the movement? How can I help the cause, from home?*

The perceived disconnect

The largest disconnect about stay-at-home moms' place in the feminist movement is the notion that feminism can only be achieved from complete financial independence and that the choices of celebrated feminists need to fit the lives of every other feminist in the movement.

According to the Merriam-Webster dictionary, the definition of feminism is quite simple:

1: the theory of the political, economic, and social equality of the sexes

2: organized activity on behalf of women's rights and interests

So, let's be clear: The act of *choosing* to stay home with your children *is* an act of feminism. Exercising your right to choose means that no one else can force you in one direction or the other. In this instance, having the equal opportunity to *choose* a course in life is the muscle behind feminism. If choice and equality are celebrated, then a mother choosing to stay home is that very theory in practice. There are no defined regulations about the details of one's choice.

Let's remind ourselves that feminism is not a one-size-fits-all existence. While feminists are often portrayed as march leaders, CEOs, and political office candidates, let's not forget that they're also stay-at-home moms—they're also *you and me*.

If you are a stay-at-home mom who believes in equal rights for women, then you are a feminist. If your core values align with the cause, you have a place in the movement. And the feminist stay-at-home mom has a big place in the movement.

The importance of stay-at-home moms in the theories of equality

Encouraging equal opportunities across political, economic, and social platforms has nothing to do with job title and everything to do with being a decent human being. By saying that feminists can only choose a life fulfilled by career is, in fact, ridding women of choice. And the power of a choice is a facet of equality. Respecting each other's personal choices and life preferences and acknowledging different values and priorities is the only way to unite together as women and stand up to injustices, together.

Stay-at-home moms are nurturing and teaching the next generation of feminists—daughters and sons—24 hours a day, 7 days a week. Stay-at-home moms have the time and brainpower to make meaningful impacts on our children and teach them the importance of equality, starting from a young age. Stay-at-home moms not only have a big place in the movement but also the future of the movement.

Feminism at home

While the children of stay-at-home moms are not witnessing their mothers out there shattering through glass ceilings in the corporate or political world, stay-at-home moms still have the power to exemplify equal rights and equal opportunities within their own homes.

Instead of looking at your time at home as a poor example of feminism, see it as the perfect opportunity to teach your children the importance of equal rights. You have your children's undivided attention all day, every day, so why not raise this next generation with the right tools to help shape their thoughts for a better, more equal tomorrow?

I've been blessed with a daughter and a son so I can exemplify the importance of equal opportunities and equal rights to both genders during these formative years.

With my daughter, I do and will continue to encourage strength and healthy competition based on her skill set, not her sex. She will know that she has the power and strength to compete with males.

With my son, I encourage the mindset that girls/women *can* compete with him. I'm not encouraging that he needs to bow down or ease up in the presence of female competition, but I am encouraging him to support, and not think twice about females, being on the same playing field as him, as equals in the competition.

This starts with laying the groundwork for equal rights and equal opportunity at home. There's no "that's a boy thing" or "that's a girl thing" in our home. My daughter and my son will both have equal opportunities to play sports, cook meals, mow the lawn, wash the dishes, and when the time comes, get a job. I'm working at empowering them both and teaching them that setting and achieving goals is not dependent on sex, but rather on personal drive and practiced skills. Hard work will be rewarded. Freebies do not exist. Equality is the norm, not the exception.

It's one thing to teach these things at home, behind closed doors, but another to empower our kids to illuminate this out in the real world. If my children encounter instances of unfairness based on gender, or race for that matter, I want them to be the ones who stand up to the injustice and set the tone for change. I need to give them the skills and knowledge to be *and* lead the reformation.

So, how am *I* participating in the movement? Where is *my* place in feminism as a stay-at-home mom? I am raising the next generation and the next big wave of change with careful intentions and guidance. Being on the home front is just as important as being on the front lines of feminism—if we're looking for the biggest influence to change the injustices around equal rights for women, we need to start by looking in our own homes and what values we're instilling in our children.

Yes, my days are filled with domestic responsibilities, but I also have a brain, the power, and the will to enthusiastically teach my children what equality looks like from the core of a family. My daughter will know that while I chose to stay home with her, she can choose whatever path she wants—full of equality and empowerment. My son will know that just because I stayed home with him does not mean that all women should be stay-at-home moms.

No, the woman's place is not in the home; it's wherever she chooses it to be and wherever she can offer the best of herself, whether that's concentrated in a career or a family.

Toolkit: Ways for stay-at-home moms to exemplify feminism

Let your children see you with a hammer, an apron, a laptop, a book, a voice—allow them to see the many hats you wear as a stay-at-home mom and a valued member of society.

Educate your children about the injustices that exist today and discuss ways on how to overcome these obstacles for tomorrow.

Ask your children if they've seen inequality at school, in sports, with their friends—help them identify it and discuss ways to rectify it.

Teach your children how to be an ambassador for equal rights at school, in extracurricular activities, and in the community.

Let your children hear your voice on the matters at hand. Express your opinion on public affairs; discuss the issues openly with your partner and your friends, in front of your children.

Attend local marches, volunteer at rallies, sign petitions, physically show up and support the cause.

Use your time at home with your children to show and teach them about the importance of equality. Just talking about it out loud speaks volumes for the cause. The change starts at home.

Exercise

List five ways you can begin exemplifying and teaching your children (at whatever age they are now) about equal rights for women.

Affirmations

- I am a strong feminist who can help make a difference in our world.
- I have an important role as a feminist and a stay-at-home mom.
- I am empowering my children by teaching and exemplifying equality.
- I am empowered by my choice to stay home.
- I am empowered to make a difference with my children, the next generation of influencers.

Section 3:
More than Mom

Chapter 11

Boosting Confidence by Nurturing Body, Mind, Soul

"You can't pour from an empty cup."
—Unknown

I sobbed into my husband's arms, "I just feel like I have nothing left to give!" The words stung my soul as they left my lips. It was a low moment in my early months as a new stay-at-home mom. Exhausted and depleted, admitting my presumed failure felt like rock bottom. I was sleep deprived and feeling lonely and lost in my new existence. I had given motherhood *everything* I had, and it seemed like it wasn't enough. I wasn't enough.

My husband is a man of few words, but he often picks the right ones: "You can't forget to take care of yourself." Such a simple suggestion but it held the key to unlocking my own happiness and, in turn, giving the best version of myself to my family.

Putting your own needs first feels selfish at first glance. Especially as a stay-at-home mom who's dedicated your entire existence to caring for your babies and your families, it feels unnatural to then turn that care inward.

I've learned over time, that way of thinking, full of guilt, is actually backward. It should be *because* you are dedicating 100 percent of your time to your family, it is *imperative* that you take care of yourself first. There's a valid reason that flight attendants instruct parents, in light of a change in cabin pressure, to secure their own oxygen masks first before securing their children's oxygen masks: You can't help anyone else if *you* can't breathe.

By failing to care for your body, mind, and soul, you won't be able to breathe. You become run-down, less patient, and physically and mentally unable to thrive in your role. The best car on the market does not work without a full tank of gas (or full battery), a light bulb cannot brighten a room unless it's powered by electricity, and a mother cannot function at her absolute best unless she is cared for, too.

....

"Making time for myself has been the hardest part. I've found I just can't give my best when I'm running on empty, so I make sure to do something just for me every day. It can be taking the time to make myself my favorite cup of tea or taking in the view of the sky from my

kitchen window. Find yourself some moments to get a breath of fresh air." —Amanda Ortega

A recent Gallup poll concluded that stay-at-home moms were significantly less likely than working moms to consider their lives "thriving" and experienced higher rates of depression.[1] And I get it, I really do. As stay-at-home moms it's easy to rationalize: *Since this is my only job, I'm going to throw 100 percent of myself into it.* And while that's great in theory, in order to give your "all," you need to take timeouts to replenish, restore, and refill, or the well will run dry. And when wells run dry, they start to crack, deconstruct, and ultimately stop functioning.

As a mother, you must make it a priority to nurture your own body, mind, and soul to keep your well full and thriving—not only for your own well-being, but for the sake of your family's.

"My hardest moment as a stay-at-home mom happened when I realized I was on the verge of depression from all the mom guilt I was burying inside my chest. My 2-year-old suddenly stopped napping and my baby was up each night cutting teeth. The house was getting messier than ever, and I desperately needed more help from my husband who was gone almost constantly. I nearly quit my writing dream in that season due to the numb feeling of hopelessness I'd begun feeling each day. It was a bitter pill to swallow, but I suddenly realized

I had to break the silence and reach out. Being honest with my husband, getting a sitter once a week to give me a chance to recharge, and the power of prayer were the three tools that got me through that difficult season." —Laura Harris

Nurturing body

The human body is really quite miraculous because it will keep going despite sub-optimal conditions. You may not even realize that you're operating at a lower level of functionality or happiness because of the adrenaline and sheer willpower that continues through your veins. However, this is not a sustainable existence. You will crash—if not physically, then mentally.

Exercise is one of the most basic needs of the human body. While exercising obviously has its physical benefits, like weight loss and muscle building, it also plays a huge part in overall health and mental well-being. Exercise is important for overall health and disease prevention and is specifically useful for run-down moms as it boosts moods, provides mental clarity, and facilitates energy.

These amazing little things called endorphins are released when the body exercises, boosting your mood and clearing your mind. Then the physical act of getting your heart rate up and your blood flowing provides a boost in energy levels. I'm a big coffee drinker, but even the strongest cup of joe doesn't compare to the energy boost I receive from even a quick workout.

So, better mood + clarity + energy sprinkled with overall health, strength, and weight loss? *Where do we sign up?*

As a stay-at-home mom, the biggest obstacle standing in the way of exercise is finding the time. Where do we make the space to squeeze in workouts from home or go to the gym while caring all day, every day for little ones? Schedules are tight and there are always a million other things to do other than workout. However, by making your health a priority (remember, not only for you, but also so you can best care for your family) exercising will become nonnegotiable. Here are a few tips on how to make exercise happen as a stay-at-home mom:

- Find a gym with a daycare. Win-win as your little one will get some playtime and peer interaction while you get in a good sweat.

- Find workout classes that incorporate babies or children. Do some research in your area to find:
  - Fit4Mom/Stroller Strides classes where kiddos are along for the ride as you exercise outside with other moms in your neighborhood.
  - Mom and baby or mom and toddler yoga classes.
  - Baby-wearing barre classes where you can actually complete a workout with your baby secure in your baby carrier.

- Workout in your home—during naps, after the kids go to bed for the night, or with your kiddos in the mix, acting as cute little weights.

Workout routines from home

Some days it's just not realistic to attend a workout class outside of the home. But, this does not mean you need to forgo your workout for the day. You can accomplish small workouts during nap times or even incorporate your kiddo(s) into your at-home workout routine.

I've rounded up some awesome workout routines and instructions for you to do from the comfort of your own home. To watch the exercise video, visit *thetribemagazine.com/best-at-home-exercise-routines-for-moms*

Energy-boosting recipes

Food also plays a big part in staying healthy and energized through our days that are chock-full of chasing tiny humans around. It's easy to slip into bad eating habits like grabbing quick, unhealthy snacks, or even worse, *forgetting* to eat throughout the day!

Make sure to include super foods and energy-boosting bites into your daily diet, such as eggs, nuts, fruits, vegetables, whole grains, fish, brown rice, beans, and legumes.

Again, as busy moms, time is of the essence! *I feel you.* I've compiled a list of energy-boosting, healthy, easy, and quick meals for you to make for *yourself* throughout the week. Grab the recipes here: *thetribemagazine.com/quick-healthy-meals-busy-moms*

Nurturing mind

Mommy brain is a real thing. First, I blamed my mental fuzziness on pregnancy, then early motherhood, then toddlers, but I think the real culprit is just motherhood in general—keeping track of your kiddos lives in addition to your own—there are just so many moving parts! As a stay-at-home mom, your mind is consumed with daily schedules, diaper changes, meal prep, and chores. Many mothers have described the fear of their brains "turning to mush" without stimulating thoughts, ideas, and regular learning taking place throughout the course of their days.

So, how to fight the mush and the laziness?

Toolkit: Exercises for your brain

The following is a list of ideas to nurture your mind throughout your days on the home front:

1. **Learn a new language.** Play a language-learning app or program in the background throughout your day. You *and* your kiddos will benefit from the lessons.

2. **Complete sudoku and crossword puzzles.** These will get your mind thinking and give you a sense of accomplishment when you solve the puzzles.

3. **Play a new sport.** This is a win-win because it will provide physical and mental exercise as you practice hand-eye coordination and new concepts and strategies for winning. (Think: tennis, golf, squash ball.)

4. **Write.** Obviously I'm biased, but writing exercises the brain and the creative bone and acts a vehicle to express your deepest thoughts. Try writing in a journal, on a blog, or begin writing a book.

5. **Read.** Reading not only exercises your brain but also transports you to a different life and world, giving you a needed break from daily routines.

6. **Memorize.** Practice memorizing things you see throughout your day: grocery lists, children's books, paragraphs in chapter books, number sequences, and so on. The exercise of committing things to memory is like taking your brain for a jog.

7. **Practice fine motor skills.** Think: sewing, knitting, painting—many of these things might even become fun new hobbies.

8. **Learn to play a musical instrument and read music.** Learning how to read music and play a new instrument will test your mind and provide you the satisfaction that comes from creating music.

Nurturing soul

While it may be easier to justify nurturing your body and mind, your soul needs some TLC, too. Soul nurturing can be expressed through whatever activities or self-care practices that make you feel good inside. Ask yourself: *What do I need in order to become the best version of myself?* Is it more sleep? Is it more alone time? Is it setting aside time to practice a new hobby or give back to your community? Identify what you need in order to set your soul on fire, then go and pursue that.

Self-care

Self-care is such a broad topic and will change based on each person's individual needs. It's also likely that your own needs for self-care will change week to week, month to month, or year to year. Sometimes you'll need more exercise and healthy eating habits, sometimes you'll need more self-pampering like a massage or getting your hair done, and sometimes you'll need much more simple things like spending time with loved ones, taking a nap, or binge-watching your favorite TV show.

Allow yourself the time and space to completely tune into your own needs. What would make you feel good right this very moment? What would make you feel alive, *right now*? Identifying your needs is half the battle, while the other half is securing the time to fill those needs.

Timeouts

As a mother, especially if you're a mother with toddlers, you're likely not a stranger to the concept of timeouts. Timeouts, as we understand them, provide a time and space for someone to remove themselves from certain situations, reset, and reflect. Taking this concept, give yourself (yes, you—the mom) timeouts. Not as a punishment for bad behavior of course, but because your soul needs the time and space to reset, recharge, and reflect. In order to do that, you need to remove yourself from your current situations.

Timeouts will exist in different forms for every person and her individual preference, so I can't tell you what your specific soul needs in order to thrive. However, I hope to inspire you to find your personal timeouts that will fill your cup back up.

The following examples are a few of my timeouts that each feed my soul in a different way—but each play an important role in my overall happiness and ability to thrive as a mom:

- **Rest.** I can function off of very little sleep and pure adrenaline (as proven throughout my son's first year of life), but I've realized I'm the worst version of myself when I'm not getting enough sleep. In the early days of life with two under two when I was getting three hours of sleep total each night, I actually hired a babysitter to come and watch my children for two hours one day so I could sleep. Yes, I had a million other things I could have done during that coveted two-hour window of freedom (the laundry was overflowing and the house was a disaster!), but during that season of life when sleep was scarce, I needed to prioritize rest. Catching up on sleep allowed me to turn around and give my all to my family again.

- **Regular manicures/pedicures.** This seems superficial at first glance, but the hour and a half I spend in a big comfy chair once every other month while someone else tends to my hands and feet—which quite literally do all the heavy lifting during the daily grit of caring for tiny humans—does wonders for recharging my soul. I leave with pretty nails, relaxed muscles, and a fresh outlook on life.

- **Writing.** My soul functions best when I can get my deeper thoughts out of my mind and out onto paper. I write during nap times, evenings, weekend mornings, whenever I can get my hands on a chunk of time that allows space for fluid thoughts.

- **Alone time.** Sometimes this means simply going for a drive and listening to loud music with the windows rolled down and a really good song on the radio. Sometimes this means taking my dog for a walk on the beach and feeling the sand in my toes and hearing the waves crash. On one occasion, I simply went through the Chick-fil-A drive-thru, ordered chicken nuggets and a chocolate milkshake, then sat in my car in the parking lot and ate and drank in complete silence. *It was glorious!* Whatever form of alone time I choose, it provides the same purpose: for me to collect my thoughts and recenter.

....

Counseling advice

"When I see a mother in my office, inevitably the topic of self-care comes up. I see the pain, the desire to evade the topic, and defenses come up.
When I ask, 'Where are you on the list [of priorities]?' the typical response is 'I'm not.' Often what we end up exploring are feelings of guilt for thinking of self-care (and the shame that comes with this

guilt), the notion that a 'good mom' is a 'wonder mom' (the mom that can, and will, do everything and do it wonderfully always), and sometimes, the belief that motherhood means sacrificing self always. Sometimes, the challenge of engaging in self-care comes from what was modeled to you as you grew up. What did it look like for your mother or father? Did they engage in self-care, too little or too much? This affects us. Another hurdle in giving yourself permission to make self a priority is a worry that your mate, family, friends expect you to give all of self to parenting. I say this gently as a response to that worry: It is not your problem what they think. That is about them, not you. If any of this feels familiar, I invite you to take a deep breath and a mental step back. Now, look at yourself through the eyes of self-compassion. I know it is sometimes the hardest thing to do. Self-compassion is really about loving-kindness, truth with gentleness, and authenticity. With that view in mind, see if there is room to embrace self-care, whether it is challenging the harsh taskmaster in your head or taking a walk or meeting with a sup-portive friend. Hopefully, all of the above and more."
—Karen Simms, mental health counselor

Exercise: Nurturing action plans

Ask yourself: What do I need *right now* in order to thrive? What do I need to fill my cup back up with so I can be the best version of myself today?

Create your path to leading a happier life with a cup full of self-care. Create a table with three columns: "Body," "Mind," and "Soul." Under each column, list ways to fill your life up in the corresponding category. Perhaps under your "Body" column, you vow to try one new healthy recipe each week and carve out three nap times per week to complete at-home workouts. Under your "Mind" column, perhaps you vow to sign yourself up for a tennis lesson, piano lesson, or simply printing out sudoku or crossword puzzles to complete throughout your week. Under your "Soul" column, perhaps you book yourself a reoccurring monthly manicure and pedicure appointment at your local nail shop, or you wake up five minutes early each morning to leave time for a meditation to start your day. Give yourself whatever you need to thrive.

Affirmations

- Taking care of myself allows me to be a better mother.
- Taking care of myself is essential for taking care of my family.
- I have the power to create the best version of myself.
- I know best what I need in order to thrive and I allow myself the space and time for self-care.
- By taking care of myself regularly, I'm providing myself with the confidence and strength to take care of my family.

Chapter 12

Redefining Your Sense of Self

"We will discover the nature of our particular genius when we stop trying to conform to our own or to other peoples' models, learn to be ourselves, and allow our natural channel to open."
—Shakti Gawain

"Bobby...Julia...Mark..." My fifth-grade teacher called each student to the front of the classroom to fetch our graded short-story essays—our final project for the year.

I had spent hours brainstorming a storyline for that particular piece of fiction, and even more time writing, erasing, and rewriting each page in perfect cursive. It was my finest work to date!

"Kristin." I sprung up from my seat.

As I reached for my paper, Mr. Scates bent down deliberately and whispered, "Excellent work. One day I'm going to hand you a book to sign for me because you're going to be an author."

Even at such a young age I stood there staggered at the weight of his words before replying, "Thank you, Mr. Scates. I would like that."

I walked back to my desk with a colossal grin, studying the large red "A+" crowning the top of my very first "book."

Writing has always been my passion, an outlet, and my preferred form of communication. I'm a mediocre public speaker, and I often can't find the appropriate words during daily interactions, but give me a laptop and a blank Word document and I will articulate the very inner workings of my thoughts and sentiments. That's just me.

After that day in Mr. Scates' class, I continued to write many more short stories, essays, and poems—some for school but mostly as an artistic exodus in my free time.

As I got older and some of the realities of the real world materialized, I recognized the challenges in earning a substantial income from writing. Consequently, I veered off my course a bit, obtaining a major in marketing followed by an ascent up the corporate ladder.

In my corporate life, writing existed for me in the form of business plans, press releases, and ad copy. Although my work was huddled under the creative umbrella, I missed being able to write outside of the branded lines—in my own voice.

Ten years into my career, my husband and I welcomed our first baby who brought animated color into our composed lifestyle. My black-and-white corporate job couldn't compete with her radiance, so I pivoted and submerged into a new existence as a stay-at-home mom.

Three months into my new role, I was already spellbound by motherhood's gamut of emotions—raw joy, confusion, excitement, exhaustion—and I had no choice but to write everything down. I was unchained from the corporate world, in the presence of a tiny muse, and had about two hours per day—during naps—to unload my thoughts onto a mommy blog.

Miraculously, other mothers began reading my words and relating to my affections. Suddenly, I had built a small community of women—new mothers—who appreciated my honesty and thanked me for articulating their feelings.

These moms who echo my mommy deliberations while navigating the open seas of motherhood are now my propeller launching me forward on my writing journey.

And here I sit, 24 years after my fifth-grade teacher planted a seed, which grew into my heart and circulated through my veins, and is making my fingers dance across a keyboard at this very moment. A passion that never died, a spark that never fizzled.[1]

Who are you?

Who are you (besides being a kickass mother, of course)?

Are you taken off-guard by this question? In your past career life, this question was probably easily answered with your job title or field of expertise, but in stay-at-home motherhood, when we set aside our "mom" title, who are we? The question might feel uncomfortable because as stay-at-home moms we often consume this role quite entirely, leaving little space for anything else to exist. As mothers we're so saturated with raising well-rounded humans that perhaps we forget to foster our own need to be well-rounded humans, too.

Possibly a startling realization for some stay-at-home moms is that they *need* an outlet outside of "mom." It might be hard to admit that "mom" is simply not enough or that your mind, heart, and soul desire something beyond that existence. Remember that you are a multifaceted person with multiple layers, interests, talents, and desires. It's what makes you unique and interesting and alive.[2]

If you notice guilt starting to bubble up to the surface with just the thought of finding yourself an outlet, combat those emotions with knowing that an outlet outside of motherhood allows you the space to become a better mother and a more well-rounded human being. By demonstrating your involvement in your own hobbies and passions, you're also showing your child/children how to lead a life worth living. Don't forget to show your kiddos all sides of you—they'll be happy to know and learn from the whole you.

Exercise: Get to know yourself again

Write down your answers to the following questions without thinking twice. Whatever pops into your head first, write it down quickly before you tell yourself what you "should" write.

1. What are you doing when you're happiest?
2. What were you doing when you laughed the hardest you've ever laughed?
3. What was the last thing you were doing when you felt on top of the world?

4. Who are the people you're hanging out with when you feel most comfortable and happy?

5. Where's your favorite place to be? (Somewhere in the mountains? A specific beach town? A favorite city?) Why do you like it there?

6. What's your favorite kind of music? What's your favorite song?

7. What's your favorite movie genre? What's your favorite movie?

8. What's your favorite kind of food?

9. What was your favorite sport or activity to do when you were younger?

10. What skill do you possess that you're really proud of?

11. What was your favorite class you've ever taken?

12. What's your lifelong dream?

Reflect

Study your answers and get to know yourself again. Perhaps your answers have changed a little bit since becoming a mother. That's fine—even more reason to get to know the new you and your new preferences.

Study your answers to questions 1–4 and brainstorm ways to recreate these great experiences. Is it hanging out with old friends who you haven't seen in a while? Is it experimenting with an old activity you haven't tried since childhood?

Study your answers to questions 5–9 and brainstorm ways to incorporate more of these things into your daily life. Plan a vacation to your favorite city, one you haven't visited in some time; make a reservation at a restaurant that serves your favorite type of food, or learn how to cook a new dish using your favorite style of food; rewatch your favorite movie; sign up for an adult's sports league in a sport that you use to enjoy back in high school.

Study your answers to questions 10–12 and brainstorm ways to continue using and practicing your skill-set that you're really proud of, further your education in a topic that really resonated with you, or create small action steps to move toward achieving your lifelong dream. (Example: *My lifelong dream has always been to write a book, so I enrolled myself in an online class exploring "how to write the best non-fiction book proposal," which lead to me creating and query-ing a book proposal, securing a literary agent, and receiving a book deal from a publisher. And now here I am, writing my first book. I can attest—small steps lead to fulfilling big dreams.*)

Identifying an outlet

Now that you've reconnected with yourself and have tuned into your likes and preferences, let's identify what types of outlets might be right for you in this new season of motherhood.

Start by giving yourself the permission to search for an outlet outside of motherhood and allowing yourself the space to express your self. Fostering passions and hobbies is a healthy practice no matter what your role in life might be. We all need the space to try new things, nurture old or new skills, and experience the rewards that different outlets provide.

Rediscover old hobbies and passions

Remember when you had hobbies? Those things that filled your soul back up because you genuinely enjoyed doing them. You made time for them in your life because they made you feel at peace or alive.

Before you became a stay-at-home mom, or even before that—before the realities of the real world materialized, what were you interested in? What did you want to be when you grew up? What topics and activities were you passionate about?

For me, I rediscovered my love for writing and started pursuing this passion every chance I got. I started a mommy blog, then an online magazine for moms, and now I'm writing a book. You can allow your own passion or hobby to grow and evolve however you'd like.

Exercise: Resurrecting old passions and hobbies

Write down 15 things you loved doing as a child, young adult, or prior to becoming a mother.

Go down your list and vow to practice or retry each thing throughout the course of the next few months to see if it's a good fit in this new season of your life.

Explore new hobbies and passions

As we grow and evolve through life, we may not like the things we use to or perhaps they don't fit right within our new lives. If you realize that all of the hobbies and passions you held prior to becoming a mom are now of little or no interest to you, that's completely fine. However, that doesn't mean that you should give up on finding an outlet outside of motherhood.

Try brainstorming new hobbies or possible passion projects that you have never experienced before. Perhaps you have some things that you've always wanted to try but never got around to them. Now's your time to explore new interests and see if they're a right fit.

Toolkit: Hobby ideas worth exploring

If you're feeling stuck on what new hobby to pursue, here are some suggestions to get you thinking:

- Dancing
  - hip-hop
  - ballet
  - ballroom
  - cultural
  - interpretive
- Learning to play a musical instrument
  - piano
  - guitar
  - flute
  - clarinet
  - drums
  - saxophone
  - trumpet
  - trombone

- Join a new sports team
  - soccer
  - softball
  - kickball
  - bowling
  - volleyball
  - flag football
- Learn a new independent sport
  - golf
  - tennis
  - squash ball
  - ping-pong
  - horseback riding
  - cooking
  - sky diving
  - hiking
  - mountain climbing
  - painting
  - cycling
  - running
  - triathlon training
  - boxing
  - karate/Tae-kwon-do
  - writing
  - skateboarding

- ○ practicing yoga and/or meditation
- ○ gardening
- ○ Pilates
- ○ water skiing/wakeboarding
- ○ snowboarding
- ○ knitting
- ○ sewing
- Enrolling in a new class (online or offline)
  - ○ writing
  - ○ photography
  - ○ graphic design
  - ○ web coding
  - ○ cooking
  - ○ foreign language
  - ○ music/instrument
  - ○ history
  - ○ theatre
  - ○ personal training

Exercise: Exploring new passions and hobbies

Write down 15 things you've always been curious about or wanted to try as a child, young adult, or prior to becoming a mother.

Go down your list and vow to try each thing throughout the course of the next few months to see if it's a good fit in this season of your life.

Affirmations

- Passions and hobbies fuel my soul, sharpen my mind, and make me a better person and mother.

- My children benefit from seeing me follow my dreams and make time for my passions and hobbies.

- I know myself and what I need in order to thrive.

- I evolve through life and am constantly reinventing myself.

- I have a passion and a curiosity for life.

- I only get one life, and I intend to make each day count.

- There's no time like the present.

Chapter 13

Nap Time Hero: Turning Your Passions into a Business

"Don't ask yourself what the world needs; ask yourself what makes you come alive. And then go and do that. Because what the world needs is people who have come alive."
—Howard Thurman

Three months into my new life as a stay-at-home mom, I walk into my daughter's nursery as she naps—half because I want to make sure she's still breathing, half because I feel lost inside of my own home.

The steady rise and fall of her little body under the swaddle and her lips parted no more than a centimeter set me at peace. I'm still in awe of her beautiful presence, and I smile because I get to be a part of something so momentous—raising a daughter.

Feeling inspired, I head into the living room, open my laptop, and double-click on the Microsoft Word icon. A blank white page pops up and the cursor blinks steadily. It feels like an invitation.

I'll write, I think. *I'll write it all.*

I began writing about my journey through motherhood as a creative outlet in the early, uncertain days of motherhood. My innocent mommy blog explored the humorous parts of raising tiny humans right along with the more trying moments. Writing felt therapeutic and a creative way for me to work through the gamut of emotions I was feeling. Readers would comment that it also felt therapeutic for them to read my words, which inspired me to keep going. My heart wasn't in it for the money; I was simply vested in writing because it was a creative outlet that filled my soul, outside of motherhood.

About a year into my writing journey, I felt the need to reach a bigger audience. I rounded up my two sisters and we launched *Tribe Magazine*, an online magazine for women. We wrote articles about anything that interested us as modern-day women: health and wellness, travel, exercise, recipes, home, career, and of course, motherhood. Again, money was never the driving factor—it was a passion project.

A year after that, my two sisters decided to pivot in their careers and both enrolled in nursing school while I had my second baby, my son. A few months into life with two under two, I felt that same urge to start writing about motherhood again. I rebranded *Tribe Magazine* into an online publication for moms only, and opened it up to contributing writers. Since then, *Tribe* has truly taken on a life of its own. I've published hundreds of mom writers and authors and have reached hundreds of thousands of moms from all over the world. *Tribe* grew into just that—a tribe of moms, raising tiny humans.

I also began submitting my writing to bigger publications and soon my work was published on the *Huffington Post*, Literary Mama, Big City Moms, Pregnant Chicken, and Red Tricycle, among other popular parenting sites. Somewhere along the line, I started taking myself seriously as a writer. What had started as a passion project and a creative exodus in my free time, turned into a new career I had built, from home. I wrote during nap times, in the evening, and on the weekends. For me, it was the perfect compliment to my life at home—a flexible creative outlet with the ability to make a little bit of money on the side.

....

"Tiny Tags started because I wanted a little something outside of my 'mom' life, but it also brought together my two passions—business and celebrating our little ones. When family would visit or I had time to myself, I worked on Tiny Tags. Working was my 'me time.'" —Melissa Clayton, owner, TinyTags.com

....

"I began freelance writing because something in me finally woke up, something that had been sleeping through years of working for a publishing company and then teaching high school. My kids stirred my creative heart in a way that the working world did not." —Jamie Sumner, writer and founder, Mom-Gene.com

....

"I started this as a creative outlet and something to honor my daughter. Something I could tell her [about] one day and I could show her how to make the bows— a mother, daughter team one day. My business is for the pleasure of doing it, [rather] than the money in my account." —Kate Heyde, owner, LittleAriesBows.com

Stay-at-home mom turned mompreneur

Taking your hobbies and passions and transferring them over to a business is not for every stay-at-home mom. I know super talented moms who could easily turn their creative endeavors into a successful business but have absolutely no interest in doing so. Don't feel pressure to start a business from your new outlet outside of mom. You can keep your outlet or hobby to yourself and be happy and fulfilled as a stay-at-home mom.

But, if the thought of becoming an entrepreneur from home interests you at all—whether it's the need or desire to create a little extra income or just exercise business skills, it can be a great way to balance your time at home.

"I needed an intellectual outlet—a way to engage my brain at a higher level than Goodnight Moon *and bedtime negotiations. I wanted to keep thinking, processing, and learning at higher levels."* —Molly Flinkman, writer, MollyFlinkman.com

"Stand-up paddleboarding yoga was a place I found just for me where I could reconnect out in nature. I would go paddleboarding where I was completely disconnected from the [responsibilities] as 'mom' and could remember who I was as a person...I love to give other moms this opportunity to come experience the reviving effects of the water, a place away from 'mom,' a space where they can experience self-care." —Sarah Eschenbach Freeman, owner, FloatingYogis.com

"The goal was to have it be a family business and has turned into much more than that. It has definitely helped me have a creative outlet outside of my daily mom duties and has also given me a way to connect with other moms. I don't know what my plan is for once my kids are in school, so I also see it as a way to stay connected to e-commerce, social media, and marketing in case I do want to go back to work eventually." —Julia Wheeler, owner, GunnandSwain.com

"I didn't initially start my blog to become a business. I just had a small vision of creating a space where all women can find common ground, encouragement, and inspiration. Mom-ing is tough and I just hope to help make it a little easier with a little humor and a lot of love." —Amanda Ortega, founder, AllThatsDarling.com

....

"Writing was always a hobby until I launched a personal finance blog in 2014 as a way of talking about parenthood and our financial journey. Soon I began earning money by writing on other websites and LOVED it. Today, we use my side income toward our goal of paying off our mortgage in under 10 years."
—Laura Harris, founder of LauraHarrisWrites.com and author of *The Stay-at-Home Mom Blueprint*

....

Toolkit: Steps on how to start a business from home

- **Consider your niche.** Take your business idea and research other businesses in your same niche. How will your business differ from your competitors? Why is your product/brand/service better or how does it fill a gap in the marketplace? Make sure your business provides specific value and is somehow unique from your competitors.

- **Identify your target market.** What do your ideal customers look like? In my marketing career I always liked to create personas for each "type" of client or customer I wanted to reach so I could fully understand the target market. Personas allow you to profile your customers by creating fictitious people who represent your different types of customers. You create an entire existence for each persona, get to know that individual, how he/she thinks, and then decide how you would go about reaching him/her. If you have five different ideal clients/customers, then you would create five fictitious characters, make up lives for each, and then determine how best to reach each one, helping shape your marketing plan.

Example: Suzy Smith is 28 years old (millennial), has a HHI of $100K and is pregnant with her first child. She lives in the suburbs of San Diego and is an elementary school teacher. Suzy is an Instagram power-user and has a lot of downtime in the summer when she's off for summer break.

Possible marketing conclusion: Instagram ad campaign concentrated in the summer months.

- **Consider your revenue stream(s).** Consider multiple revenue streams when designing your business. If you make and sell T-shirts for moms, consider selling them on your own website, Etsy, and Facebook, and providing them wholesale to brick and mortar shops.

  If you start a blog, look into ad networks, sponsored post opportunities, writing a guide or an e-book available for purchase, or selling complimentary apparel in your niche.

- **Build the bones (website/branding).** Set up a website and a domain. If you want a turnkey option, begin selling your products on Etsy, which provides a built-in platform and checkout process.

  Hire a graphic designer to help you with branding, or create your own with free sites like Canva or PicMonkey.

- **Write a business plan.** Business plans help you identify your niche, your customers, your products or
  services, and finding a path to reaching your customers and producing revenue. Look for a business plan
  template online to help inspire your own. Sites like
  *www.score.org/resource/business-plan-template-start-
  up-business* provide a step-by-step template that you can
  download and fill in with your business information.

- **Write a marketing and public relations plan.** As a
  part of your business plan, come up with a marketing
  and PR strategy. Maybe you start with free marketing
  and PR options like content creation, social media,
  and email marketing. Start social channels for your
  business, especially those that your target demo-
  graphic uses daily. Start connecting and interacting
  with your target market on a regular basis.

  As you start bringing in some income, consider
  paid marketing options like Facebook and Instagram
  ads, sponsored posts with influencers who reach
  your target market, sponsorships with local events,
  ad word campaigns, ads on websites or publications
  that your target market reads, and so on.

- **Network—online and offline.** Meeting other like-
  minded mom entrepreneurs in person and online will
  result in some great inspiration, tools, and resources,
  best practices, and support through your business
  journey. Plus, the women you'll connect with know
  what it's like to run a business and be a mom at the
  same time. Join mom entrepreneur groups online

(search for Facebook groups in your niche—"Boss Moms" is one of my favorites), and offline meet-ups that offer monthly meetings, speakers, and networking events or larger, yearly conferences.

- **Work smarter with automation.** Since you'll likely be a one-woman show in the beginning, find ways to automate your business so you don't waste your time with tedious tasks. Look into helpful resources for small businesses:

  - **Buffer** or **Hootsuite** measure important social media analytics and schedule social posts across multiple platforms.

  - **Tailwind** automatically schedules your pins for Pinterest at the most optimal times when your followers are on the network and ready to pin. (And Pinterest itself can be such a big traffic driver for your website!)

  - **IFTT** can automate social media and life in general. For example, you can make a rule that if you post a photo and caption to Instagram, then the image and text will also push live on your Twitter feed. Or, you can make a rule to save all photos you've been tagged in on Facebook to your iOs. You can even arrange for the weather for the following day to be emailed to you daily at 5 p.m. This tool is truly your right-hand woman.

  - **Dasheroo** allows you to access all of your business analytics on one platform, including your

Google analytics from your website, MailChimp stats from your email campaigns, and all of your social media reach and interactions.

○ **Click Funnel** takes viewers who are reading your content and seamlessly transfers them into your predetermined sales funnel.

○ **PayPal** or **QuickBooks** are helpful for sending and receiving invoices.

○ **Bookify** is perfect for small business accounting and bookkeeping needs.

○ **Trello** and **Evernote** are great for tracking tasks and projects from idea to completion through admin-type functions.

Best advice for starting your own business

Because I always receive so much inspiration from my mom peers, I asked some fellow stay-at-home moms/mompreneurs to offer up their best piece of advice for other moms wanting to start their own business from home:

- *"Always support other women! Even those seen as competitors because you never know where a connection will lead you. Join networking groups, find other mompreneurs, and surround yourself with uplifting and supportive people. Celebrate the small wins, take each day as it comes and be proud of your hard work!"* —Ashley Wilson, founder, KeepCalmandWineOn.com

- *"Think about your why. If your why is to be home with your baby, then don't start a brick-and-mortar business that will require you to be away. If your why is to make a million dollars, make sure that you have the time you will need to ramp up that business. Have a plan for how you plan to get the work done."* —Lisa Druxman, founder, Fit4Mom.com

- *"NETWORK. I have found other business people, especially other mom entrepreneurs, to be the most supportive group around. We share frustrations and wins and ideas. I owe my business to the other moms who have supported me in this venture!"* —Julia Wheeler, owner, GunnAndSwain.com

- *"Be sure to follow your heart and to take time for yourself."* —Bri Grajkowski, owner, BriGeeski.com

- *"As a mom and business owner, you're constantly serving others. Remember to be kind to yourself, too. When you design your schedule, specifically carve out time for rest and recovery. If you really allow yourself to replenish, you'll be a more patient mom, you'll offer a higher quality service, you'll be sharper, more optimistic, healthier, and overall more lucrative."* —Brittany Marker, Reading Elephant at ReadingElephant.com

- *"Hire a sitter! Even if it's just one morning a week. You can try your best to work when the baby naps or to wake up extra early, but then life happens and your child goes through a rough transition and the house is a mess and you're propping your eyelids up with toothpicks. Having one pocket of time JUST for your business will help immensely."* —Laura Harris, founder of LauraHarrisWrites.com and author of *The Stay-at-Home Mom Blueprint*

- *"Start small and lay the foundation when your kiddies are little. Find five hours a week to do something you love that could become a business. Then as your kiddies start to go to preschool and you have more time, you can build upon what you started. I started Tiny Tags when my second son was born, and I worked about five to 10 hours a week on it. By the time my third son was born, Tiny Tags was gaining momentum and making money. My husband was happy to support me, and I would start to work on the weekends when he was home and at night. The idea of starting a business is overwhelming, but if you start small it is a lot easier to manage."* —Melissa Clayton, owner, TinyTags.com

How to be a good stay-at-home mom and mompreneuer

The thought of running a small business on top of taking care of your kiddos full time might seem daunting. But, it is possible to achieve the best of both worlds as a stay-at-home mom and mompreneur. Here are a few tips:

1. **Start small.** Don't expect to create and run a huge business right out of the gate. Unless you're arranging outside childcare from the start, you won't be able

to dedicate the amount of time needed to building a successful business from the ground up. Set realistic expectations based on the amount of free time and resources you have available.

2. **Decide what you want from this business endeavor.** You can set parameters around how much time and effort you want to put into your business. Ask yourself if you want this to be a side business that you work on during naps and some evenings, or do you see this becoming a true part-time or full-time job, requiring hiring a nanny or looking into daycare options? Perhaps it starts as a nap time passion project and turns into a full-time business. As you grow your business, keep in mind the lifestyle that you want to maintain throughout the process. For me, I've kept my writing and *Tribe Magazine* a side-project because it was still important for me to be a stay-at-home mom to my kids and be there with them through these baby and toddler years. I work during nap times, evenings, and have hired a babysitter to watch the kiddos one morning per week. Those are my parameters that foster the lifestyle I want to maintain through having a business and being a mom. Make sure to identify and protect the type of lifestyle you want for your own life, too.

3. **Create balance.** *Ah,* balance, we meet again. If you are teetering your time between caring for your children and your business, make sure to maintain balance

and practice being present in each role. When you're with your kids, make sure to be present with them in those moments. Reading emails or taking phone calls all day while also taking care of your kids will result in not being fully present for either job. Identify what times you can/will work during the day and what times you'll dedicate to your children. Perhaps you'll vow to work during nap time and the one hour during the day that you allow your children to watch their favorite TV show. But anything outside of those work times is dedicated mommy time. Find a schedule and balance that works for you.

Affirmations

- I design my life with intention and choose what's best for my family and me, above all.
- I can be a boss and a mom.
- I am a strong, capable woman who has the power to launch a business.
- I have the power to manage my home, my family, and a business.

Chapter 14

Out of the Transition

*"There is no way to be a perfect mother,
and a million ways to be a good one."*
—Jill Churchill

There will be a day when you wake up one morning and find yourself functioning at full capacity in your new role as a stay-at-home mom. You will be caring for your precious kiddos, keeping your household running and in order, taking care of yourself by scheduling your "me time," and it will all just click. You'll suddenly realize that you're not transitioning into the role of a stay-at-home mom anymore; you are encompassing that role quite entirely, intentionally, and purposefully.

....

"I am so grateful to be able to stay at home with my babies and watch them grow. I still work, I just don't

get paid for it. Being a stay-at-home mom is by far the best job that I have ever had!" —Michelle Nelson

You are now a stay-at-home mom through and through. And you're happy. Sure, there are hard days, but there are more happy, fulfilling days. You've trained your thoughts how to make the best of trying situations and you battle any mom guilt with truth: You are a good mom.

"Every time there's been a milestone, whether it was their first step, or first cut, I have had the privilege to be there to celebrate or help make things right for them." —Amanda Ortega

You know in your heart and soul that this is where you're supposed to be at this moment in time. This existence has settled into your bones and it suits you. Of course, you might choose to go back into the workforce someday—based on your unique journey through life. But for now, you're comfortable right where you're at.

"When I decided to stay home for good when my second son was about six months old, I felt so lucky to be with my boys each day, to have this consistency where I knew what their day had been like yesterday, and where I could feel confident that they knew I was going to be there for them." —Lorren Lemmons

You look down at your growing kiddos and you reflect: They've changed you. You've changed you. You are the best version of yourself for them and for you. This is what happiness is. This is what a life well-lived looks like.

....

"I've also appreciated being the liaison between my husband and our daughter during his long hours away at work. I capture her words, actions, and special moments through picture and video, so I can give him the best possible perspective into his child's life before he gets home, long after she's been put to bed." —Marisa Svalstedt

....

But the journey doesn't stop here. The transition is over, but the rest of your life awaits. As your children continue to grow and thrive, you'll continue to grow as a mother, too. At each stage, they'll need different things from you, and you'll learn how to be there for them and for you as your family evolves, together. Remember to keep asking yourself the hard questions, digging into your soul and uncovering your truths and what makes you happy and fulfilled. As a family leader, you set the tone. Channel your happiness and watch it permeate through your family.

....

"I truly appreciate their smiles and their tales at the end of the day from everything we did." —Kate Heyde

....

Know that you have the power to continue designing a life for yourself and your family that tributes your values and goals. And when new obstacles arise (they will) and life becomes overwhelming (it will), focus on your soul's North Star, the reasons why you became a stay-at-home mom in the first place, and continue carving out your unique path through motherhood and beyond.

....

"I completely appreciate being home with my kids when they are not feeling well or when they really just want to be with their mommy. I've loved that I get to be with them to see all of their firsts and to watch them grow." —Bri Grajkowski

....

....

Counseling advice
"One of the words Kristin used to describe her decision to be a stay-at-home mom was 'pivot.' What I like about this word is it that it speaks to a change: change of scenery, point of view, idea, and meaning. Throughout this book, Kristin guided you, the reader, the mom choosing to say home, through the many pivots this next step of your journey takes you. The constant throughout, however, was the solid foundation comprised of learning to engage in self-compassion, embracing your worth, and showing up with intention, love, and mindfulness. Often, we forget the solidity of this foundation as some word or event or thought causes

turbulence in our self-worth or our self-compassion. In these moments, give space to pause, take a deep breath, feel your feet on the ground of your foundation, and remember your intentions and your love in this wonderfully hard and meaningful work. Embrace the many small pivots that give you a new scene, point of view, idea, and meaning." —Karen Simms, mental health counselor

Affirmations

- I am exactly where I am supposed to be.
- Happiness and fulfillment exude from my role as a stay-at-home mom.
- I am confident and proud of my role as a stay-at-home mom.
- I am providing the very best for my family.
- My life is beautiful and thriving.
- I am the best version of myself, right now.
- I work hard and lead a life worth living.
- I wake up with purpose and go to sleep with fulfillment.

Conclusion

A Time to Thrive

"With every choice you create the life you'll live;
with every decision you design it."
—Mollie Marti

From the moment our children are born, all we want is for them to thrive. It starts with the basics: nourishment, healthy bowel movements, enough sleep. Then you add developmental, social, and cognitive skills. Next come behavioral hurdles and the simple question you keep asking yourself as you toss in bed at night: "Are they turning into good humans?"

The requirements for "thriving" children continue to accumulate over time, so we, as mothers, make the big decisions, give every ounce of ourselves, guide them through each new milestone, accomplish small miracles that often get swept up with "routine," all while keeping tabs on the ingredients needed to raise children who are thriving. All because we want to see them thrive in life.

And what about you, Mama? Are you thriving in life?

After all the care and energy that's directed towards raising children—a breadth of strength, love, patience, and unwavering dedication—how are you filling your cup back up? What is fueling your journey through motherhood?

Leaving a career sustained by external rewards and praise, and emerging into a new existence as a stay-at-home mom— a role that requires internal strength and self-reliance—is a momentous lifestyle change. I hope this book allowed you the space and gentle reminder to flip your lens inward during this season of transition and self-discovery, and realize what you need in order to be the best version of yourself.

Intended as a roadmap offering guidance from a life based on a career to a life at home with children, this book has focused on common difficulties that stay-at-home moms face, tools and insight on how to overcome those adversities, and encouragement for inner strength and peace along the way.

Toolkit recap: 13 ways to thrive during the transition from a career to a stay-at-home mom

1. Leaving your career to start anew as a stay-at-home mom requires a leap of faith. But before you jump, it's necessary to weigh your circumstances, values, and

self in the decision making process so you choose the path that's right for you and your family.

2. Once you decide to veer off the career track and stay home with your children, it's essential to close the chapter on your past work life and redirect your attention to your present role as a stay-at-home mom. By leaving some of yourself behind—the parts that have no place or importance in motherhood, and keeping your best strengths and traits close to your heart as you move forward in your new role, you're setting yourself up for success and happiness.

3. Laying a solid foundation for your time at home by outlining your intentions and goals from the start will provide you with a place of center as you continue transitioning to life as a stay-at-home mom. Remember to revisit these intentions and goals often, and especially during times of self-doubt.

4. Your relationships with your partner, your close friends, and family members will change as you pivot from a career to life on the home front. By prioritizing one-on-one time with your loved ones, including them in your new life at home with your kids, and keeping open lines of communication, you'll be able to foster these important relationships and help them flourish through the change.

5. It's important (and even cathartic) to acknowledge some of the hardships that are associated with raising tiny humans 24/7. By placing a spotlight on these adversities, you can learn ways to overcome them

with "reset buttons," controlling your thoughts and reactions, and reminding yourself to look through the chaos and uncover the magic found in raising a family.

6. The role of a stay-at-home mom fits each of us differently. Find power in bucking the old stereotypes associated with the title, and carve out your own identity in this life. Find the balance you need in order to thrive by prioritizing your tasks and responsibilities, leaving room for an outlet outside of "mom," and asking for help when needed.

7. Be open to starting new friendships with other moms. You'll need this tribe of women throughout motherhood for support, encouragement, or simply as confirmation that you're not the only one going crazy sometimes. Actively look for new mom friends and, when you find them, nurture meaningful relationships with these women. These ladies are your people.

8. Find your own self-worth, confidence, and encouragement from within instead of seeking those necessities from some outside entity or through a paycheck. The hard work you do every day, caring for your children and your home, matters. You matter. Remember to give yourself a pat on the back from time to time because you are a *good* mom.

9. Take the destructive comments and stereotypes that you've heard about stay-at-home moms and toss them aside; there's no room for falsities in your soul.

Replace these negative outside opinions with your own truth: You are a valuable member of society who works hard at leading a family and raising members of our next generation. As soon as you come to peace with this path you've chosen, outside words or thoughts won't affect you. You'll realize the "mommy wars" between working and stay-at-home moms stem from insecurities on both sides of that coin. We need to lift each other up, not tear each other down. Every mother has her own unique journey through parenting, and we all make the best choices for our own families and circumstances. Let your soul rest in peace knowing you've made the best choice for your own family.

10. The stay-at-home mom has a big place in the feminist movement. Just because you're not shattering through glass ceilings in the corporate world doesn't mean you can't make a difference for the cause starting from the core of your own family. You have the power to raise your children to know and practice equality in everyday life.

11. By nurturing your own body, mind, and soul through exercise, mind stimulation, and self-care, you're making yourself whole again. And when you're whole, you're thriving, and your family is whole and thriving. Your family's happiness and well-being starts with your example, so don't be afraid to take some time to care for yourself.

12. Get to know yourself again—resurrect some of your buried passions or entertain new areas of interest—and give yourself the space and time to identify and nurture an outlet outside of "mom." You need this soul food.

13. If entrepreneurship interests you, explore starting your own business based on your newly identified outlet or passion. Whether you start a home business to make some extra income, as a fun hobby, or to keep your business skills up to date, as long as it makes you feel alive and thriving, it's a good way to balance your time at home.

• • • • • • • •

Mamas, if you take one thing away from this book, let it be this: Make this journey through stay-at-home motherhood your own. Only YOU have the answers to the questions you pose, the validation and self-worth you seek, and the happiness and fulfillment you desire. Stay in tune with yourself through the course of motherhood, because you have all the tools to create a beautiful life. Stay kind to yourself, true to your values, and prosper in the simple knowledge that what you do every day, raising tiny humans, matters.

Embrace this season of motherhood as a time to thrive.

Notes

Chapter 8

1. D'vera Cohn, Gretchen Livingston, and Wendy Wang. "Public Views on Staying at Home vs. Working." *Pew Research Center,* Chapter 4, 2014. *www.pewsocialtrends.org/2014/04/08/chapter-4-public-views-on-staying-at-home-vs-working/*

2. Kristin M. Helms. "Life Without Raises and Praises." *The Stay-at-Home Mom Survival Guide,* July 24, 2016, *http://thestay-at-home-momsurvivalguide.com/2016/07/life-without-raises-praises.html*

Chapter 9

1. Jon Acuff. *Start: Punch Fear in the Face, Escape Average, and Do Work That Matters.* Ramsey Press, April 22, 2013.

2. Don Miguel Ruiz and Janet Mills. *The Four Agreements: A Practical Guide to Personal Freedom (A Toltec Wisdom Book).* Amber-Allen Publishing, November 7, 1997.

Chapter 10

1. Kristin M. Helms, "We Are Girls." *The Stay-at-Home Mom Survival Guide*, December 18, 2016, *http://thestay-at-home-momsurvivalguide.com/2016/12/we-are-girls.html*

Chapter 11

1. Kristin M. Helms. "After Page One: Cycles." *Literary Mama*, June 6, 2016, *www.literarymama.com/blog/archives/2016/06/after-page-one-cycles-4.html*

2. Lydia Saad Mendes and Kyley McGeeney. "Stay-at-Home Moms Report More Depression, Sadness, Anger." Gallup, May 18, 2012. *www.gallup.com/poll/154685/stay-home-moms-report-depression-sadness-anger.aspx*

About the Author

Kristin M. Helms is the founder and editor-in-chief of *Tribe Magazine,* an online publication that reaches moms from all over the world and connects them by exploring the heart and soul of motherhood, through words. She has been published on numerous parenting sites including Literary Mama, Big City Moms, Pregnant Chicken, and Huffington Post. When her daughter was born in 2013, Helms traded her power suits and office with a view for yoga pants and life on the home front. Her transformation from corporate marketing life to stay-at-home mom has been a riotous journey, brimming with unexpected emotions, self-discovery, and the most beautiful moments of her life. Helms lives in San Diego, California, with her husband and two spirited toddlers.